Coping with Grief

The Anti-Guide to Infant Loss

For Sam and Iris

Contents

To everyone but a few,
It's just another day.
Why would they know
6 months ago,
I found you stiff and grey.

The world's gone on around me
Some days I even smile.
But my heart's forever broken,
Since the day that I lost Kyle.

"Six Month Angelversary"

By Karla Roy

Founder of the Empty Arms Foundation

Introduction

In August 2010 I lost my seven week old son, Toby, to Sudden Infant Death Syndrome. A week before he died I wrote a status and said that I was "unnaturally paranoid of SIDS." Six people commented and told me that everything would be "fine" and not to worry. I didn't know it then, but that was actually the beginning of my journey through Hell. Everything *wasn't* fine and they were wrong. We couldn't really have known that, though.

What followed was a circus of feelings, emotions, and events that I never would have dreamed possible. I was the ringmaster under a curtain that had no padlocks on any of the animals' cages. It was a nightmare. Sometimes I still feel like I am trying to wake up from it. Having no frame of reference for my grief I tried watching movies about death, reading books about it, and joining online support groups. I visited psychics and astrologers and tried to learn astral projection so that I could visit my now dead son. I cried and screamed and cut myself and drank when I was able to hold down any alcohol. I slept a lot. I lost almost all of my friends and sank into a deep depression. I scoured bookstores and the internet for advice on helping me cope. None of them helped. The spiritual ones made me feel uncomfortable. The life affirmative ones made me mad. The ones written by therapists *really* made me mad. Nobody seemed to understand my grief or my anger. They either thought I should be grateful that my child was in a "better place" or dissected my grief in such a way that it sounded clinical and pristine. Although I found that some were helpful (like *The SIDS Survival Guide*) to many of these people and books, my grief was something that could be categorized and analyzed and I was merely following steps and patterns that millions of people had followed before me.

I didn't want my loss to feel that way. My son was a person. My grief was real. It couldn't be summed up in a chapter in a psychology textbook. It was so much more complicated than what those books made it sound like.

I took to blogging which had mixed results. Sometimes I would post a dozen entries before I ever saw a single comment. Other times I would post an entry and it would create so much drama that it worsened my depression and anxiety. I felt as though people were watching my every move, just hoping I would do something wrong. Everyone seemed to have an opinion on how I *should* be handling things.

I finally discovered a network of fellow bereaved parents who I credit to literally saving my life. Through these folks (mostly women) I was able to share my grief in a way that I hadn't before. They understood my anger. They understood my fear. They understood my paranoia. They even understood the bouts of happiness that I had which sometimes made me feel worse than the bad feelings. I still felt crazy but at least I realized that I wasn't the only one in the nuthouse and that was comforting in its own way.

I'm not an expert on grief. I'm not an expert on infant loss-only on my *own* infant's loss. Unfortunately, there is no instruction book to help you through losing your child. I mean, there *are* books out there and some of them are actually helpful, but there really are no instructions for this kind of thing. We're all kind of playing it by ear.

In this book I wanted to share some of my experiences and some of the experiences of my friends in an attempt to make some kind of sense of the events and feelings that followed the loss of our infants. We don't always make sense. It's not always easy to follow our lines of thinking. And we're not even always sad. But we are always missing our children and we're all really just kind of feeling our ways along.

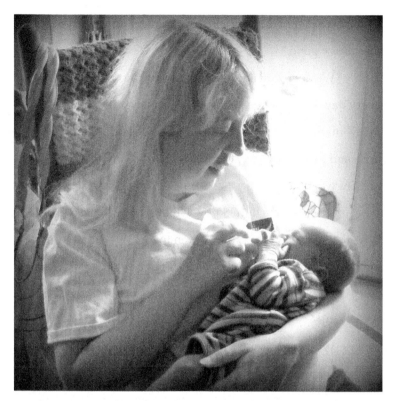

Feeding Toby

Dear family, friends, doctors, and strangers:

We belong to a group that is diverse in ethnicities, ages, social

statuses, income levels, and nationalities. Although some of us

4

have never met, we are all connected by something horrible: Our infants are gone.

We deal with a range of emotions, thoughts, and feelings every day. We no longer know how to answer the question "How many children do you have?" We have clothing, books, toys, and furniture in our homes and storage units that we have no idea what to do with.

Grief centers don't know what to do with us. They place us with pregnancy loss groups, even though we didn't lose our infants during pregnancy. Some of us have even been turned away from other child loss groups because our children were "only babies."

We have learned to be very understanding although that understanding hasn't always been reciprocated. We were understanding as friends and family disappeared in the days, weeks, and months following our children's deaths. We were understanding when the invitations to parties, dinners, movies, and get-togethers stopped. In the meantime, we sat in silent houses by ourselves, surrounded by memories that weren't always good.

We were understanding when friends couldn't come to the visitation or funeral and a year later, when we still hadn't seen them even though they lived all of ten minutes away, we still tried to understand.

We've been understanding as we listened to religious explanations that we may or may not have agreed with, to well meaning "advice," and to the inevitable comparisons that were made to the loss of your grandmother, parent, or dog.

When we weren't understanding, we were chastised and made to feel guilty. So we learned to keep our feelings to ourselves. We learned early on that people felt uncomfortable about what had happened to our children so we refrained from talking about them and their deaths, although we wanted to talk about them more than anything. We faked smiles, pretended to be in good spirits, and forced ourselves to be social though there were days when it was all we could do to force ourselves out of bed.

We have discovered that we don't get the same medical care that we used to. If our children are ill, we find that it's not always easy to convince medical professionals that there is something wrong with them. We will forever be labeled as somewhat paranoid and doctors always look at us with a little bit of skepticism. When we have serious health issues, we are sometimes treated disrespectfully and told that they are "psychological" and that we are just "sensitive" because of what happened in the past.

And speaking of doctors, it would be nice if they would utilize the thirty seconds that it would take to glance at our charts to become familiar with our history. When asked how many pregnancies we've had and how many "living children" we have, it's difficult when people assume that the "missing child" was a stillborn or miscarriage. It's hard for us to have to correct everyone on this every single time. Learn who we are.

We've indignantly listened as people accused us of being "jealous" over the fact that they have a living child. The fact is, we are not jealous of your baby-we don't want YOUR baby. We want ours back.

What we DO envy, however, is your innocence. We watch and listen as you innocently put your babies to sleep every night, sure that nothing bad will happen to them. There might even be a small part of you that thinks that we must have done something wrong, because the idea that a child can die for apparently no reason is simply too horrific and unfathomable. You put them down for naps or put them to sleep in separate rooms from you, feeling secure in the fact that they will wake up in a few hours.

We will never feel that way again.

We wish that we could have that back. We submit to checking our other children every few minutes to see if they are breathing, buying energy drinks to keep ourselves awake while our children sleep, purchasing monitors that will alarm when the breathing stops, and having panic attacks when we think we detect unnatural stillness.

We have become used to being the topics of conversations, although few people dare to venture the topic of our children. Our stories are passed around to friends, family members, and even strangers as fodder for conversation. People speculate about our mental health, our grieving process, and our family life as casually as they talk about the weather. We've had status updates, Tweets, blog entries, text messages, and even short stories written about us. In some ways, we've become a type of celebrity, as though what happened to us was so bad that it's up for public display.

While some of us were lucky enough to have paramedics, social workers, doctors, coroners, investigators, and funeral directors that were compassionate and understanding, others were not. Some of us submitted to humiliating investigations in which personal items were taken from our homes, friends and family members were interviewed, and social workers came to "teach" us how to take care of our remaining children. Some of us were allowed to ride in the ambulances with our babies, touch them, and even hold them one last time. Others were immediately treated as criminals and kept separated from their child's body until the funeral.

We have been told that "at least" we have memories of our child. We would rather have our child. And not all of our memories are good ones. Intermixed with the memories of our children smiling, cooing, and cuddling with us are the memories of their funeral, how they looked when we discovered them, and for some of us, they way that they felt when their once warm bodies became lifeless.

We also feel guilty. We feel guilty that we can't always be good partners to our spouses, that we aren't there for our friends as much as we used to be, and that we don't always have the energy to play with our remaining children. Sometimes, the guilt is worse than our sadness.

Please don't mistake our tenacity for doing well. Yes, we still manage to get up every morning (or most mornings), go to work, drive our cars, and take care of our families. We do these things because we have to. It doesn't mean that we are "over it", that we have "moved on", or that we aren't sad.

We greatly appreciate those of you who have stuck around, talked to us, cooked us meals, and continued to be our friends. We don't know what to say to you but "thank you" and we hope that's enough for now. We've seen a lot of kindness and generosity and those things have made our time bearable.

We are doing the best that we can. While it might not seem to you like we are always handling things in the best

9

manner, please remember that there are no manuals for these things. You can look at your grief charts, talk pop psychology to us, and refer us to books by other people who have dealt with loss but at the end of the day we're all individuals and we handle things in our own ways. They may not be the way that you think that you would handle them, but hopefully you will never be in our shoes and have to find out.

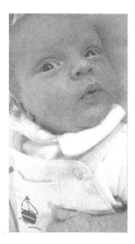

Toby

What You Might Expect After Losing Your Infant

It's important to have realistic expectations for yourself if you lose your child. Your friends, family, doctors, and co-workers will have other expectations, some which won't be reasonable at all. You'll probably find at some point that you're your own best cheerleader and gauge of feelings. So what might you expect to think, feel, and do?

You can probably count on the fact that:

You'll spend the first couple of weeks/months in a heightened sense of panic and emotion yet the "real" grief might not even start until about six months down the line.

Your grief will change over time. It might get better for awhile and then worse again. It's not linear.

You'll feel tired a lot. Grief is exhausting.

You might show physical signs of grief, not just emotional ones.

You might feel isolated and lonely and feel like people have abandoned you.

You will grieve for things that never happened or never got the chance to happen as much as you grieve for the things that did.

You might feel totally inappropriate responses to some things and that might make you feel guilty.

Your grief might bring up old issues with people and things from the past.

You might feel anger and rage at the way people treat you and lash out at others, even if you haven't been particularly sensitive in the past.

You might have suicidal thoughts.

You might not want to die but would welcome going to sleep for a long, long time.

You might find yourself losing control and crying at inopportune moments for reasons that you don't even understand.

12

You might have trouble with your memory. (I once put my keys in the microwave and my Hot Pocket in my purse.)

You might have trouble watching movies that you enjoyed in the past, especially if they involve children.

You might have panic attacks.

You might experience a conflict of faith or a sudden interest in religion where you didn't have one before.

You might have trouble leaving the house or being around large groups of people.

People will probably say things to you that are inappropriate and sometimes flat out mean.

You might go days without crying and then spend an entire weekend in bed.

You might lose patience with your other children, even though it makes you feel terrible.

You might have an increased sex drive.

You might not want to be touched at all.

Getting the News

My child died while I slept peacefully in another room. I have no idea if he cried out in his sleep or struggled to breathe or was scared. I don't even know his time of death. We estimate it to be somewhere between 3:00 am and 6:00 am since he didn't wake up for his last bottle. I didn't find him until after 9:30. When I woke up and found a quiet house I used the time to take a shower and apply makeup, sure that he would wake up any minute and I would end up looking as ragged as I usually did. I was happy for the "me" time. I will never know if I had gotten to him before my shower or foundation if I could have saved him.

I knew that my son was dead as soon as I saw him. The horror that filled me was primal. I immediately started giving him CPR. It was no use. He was as stiff and cold as a doll. After a few minutes of pumping on his chest, trying not to break his

14

little ribs, I ran down the stairs and screamed at my mother, "He's dead, he's dead!"

For a brief moment in the ambulance the heart monitor moved. I think it was just a reflex. There was no saving my son. Getting the news that your infant has died is such a horror filled moment that there is no way to describe it. The emotions I felt all at once (anger, rage, denial, adrenalin induced euphoria) would be enough to have anyone committed if you felt all of those on a regular basis. It was a nightmare.

My son died at home. He seemed healthy. Although he was a preemie, he was growing well and eating good and doing all the things he was supposed to be doing. We had no idea that when he went to sleep that night he would never wake up.

The doctor told me that Toby was dead only minutes after walking into the room and walking back out. It was official then, but I knew it long before then. I had held his hand and touched him. I knew there was no life in him. Hearing someone else say it, though, was a punch in the gut. When it was only me who knew he was dead, I could kind of find hope that maybe it wasn't real. When someone else knew it and voiced it, though, it became a reality.

April's experience

*My daughter was five months old when she died. She was a beautiful,
lively little girl and was just really starting to sit up on her own. She
had a huge personality and almost never cried. She was also my first
child. I wanted to have a dozen more after I had her because I loved her
so much. On the night she died she wasn't feeling well. She didn't have
a fever or anything but her tummy was gurgling a lot and she needed
constant burping. I was finally able to lay her down at about midnight.
I went to bed and got up and checked on her a couple of hours later. She
was fine. The next morning, though, when I woke up the house felt
different. The sun was different. My bedroom was brighter. I knew that
it was later than it should be. I was shocked when I looked at the alarm
clock and saw that it was after 10:00 am. There was a sinking feeling in
the pit of my stomach that told me something was wrong. She had
never slept like that before. I got up and raced to her bedroom but she
was already cold and gone. She had died in her sleep. I called 911 and
my mother and, on the way to the hospital, I called my husband to come
and meet us. He was working out of town that week. They pronounced
her dead upon arrival.*

Seeing their body

Some parents never see the deceased bodies of their infants until the funeral viewing. Some were able to spend time with them in the hospital before they passed away. Others, like me, discovered death long after it happened.

Seeing your baby's formerly healthy, pink, soft and warm body in death is horrifying. When I found Toby he was cold and slightly blue. By the time I left him in the hospital the blood was pooling and he looked bruised. His little face was splotchy. What wasn't red and blue was solid white. He did not look like my baby. I was dismayed by his appearance but I didn't want to look away from him. In fact, I took a picture of his body because I wanted to remember every single moment of his existence, even in death.

I remember getting incredibly angry because someone I knew entered the room with us and rather than sitting in a chair or standing they perched on the edge of the hospital bed where his body was. When they sat down, his body jiggled. I wanted to scream and punch someone. I couldn't say a word.

Some parents don't want to see their babies in this condition and I don't blame them. Others want to hold them and

17

care for them, just as they did when they were alive. There is no right or wrong way to feel. As with anything in grief, you need to go with your gut feelings and do what is best for you.

What I felt when looking at my son's body

1. Anger that the blood was running from his nose and messing up his little face.
2. Horror that that the tape and breathing tube were still on him. I wanted to take them off but didn't want to get in trouble or tear his skin.
3. Afraid that I would do something wrong and the police would come after me.
4. Ashamed that his diaper hadn't been changed and might be full.
5. Sad that he was sleeping in the same outfit he had worn all day the previous day.
6. Upset that he might be cold.
7. Antsy that I couldn't just pick him up and hold him.
8. Horrified at the different colors his body was turning.
9. Hungry because I hadn't eaten that morning.
10. Upset because we'd had a nice day planned and now it was ruined.

11. Nervous because I didn't know who was out there in the waiting room entertaining my three year old and I didn't want anyone to be inconvenienced.

12. Upset and embarrassed that I didn't feel like I was crying enough. What would people think? Surely I should be throwing myself on the floor in tears.

As you can see, some of these things didn't make sense. Oh, if you could have only been inside my head. Actually, you probably wouldn't have wanted to be. It was a mess in there. I was appalled that I felt selfish anger-anger that I was looking forward to spending a nice day out with the kids and now it was ruined. I felt like I must be the most terrible person in the world. And why was I not crying my heart out? Did I no longer have a heart? What was wrong with me?

Now, of course, I know that the only thing wrong with me was that I was in the middle of suffering the most horrific blow a parent can experience. The brain has no idea how to handle such a thing so it just goes haywire and does a little bit of everything. There is no rhyme or reason as to what goes through it, and what doesn't. You suddenly have no control over your thoughts and feelings and emotions. You have no control over your body at all.

Wanda's experience

We chose not to embalm Lindsey because of the cremation but it was offered. It made for an interesting viewing, as she still had her blood in her body, so she her fingers and toes had blackened areas almost, like where blood had pooled I guess and since she was kinda on her side when I found her, she had I think what they call blood staining where the blood pooled on that side. None of that was really "fixed" for the viewing because she wasn't embalmed and didn't get her body flushed out but they did a good job with the makeup. She also had chux under her hat and clothes to catch the oozing from her autopsy, so when I tried to pick her up or touch her you'd kinda here that chux crinkling.

When it doesn't happen at home

Some of my friends lost infants who were in daycare or at someone's house at the time of their death. Their experiences were different than mine. They dropped off perfectly healthy children to the people they trusted and went on to work, only to receive phone calls later informing them of the terrible thing that had happened.

The guilt that we suffer from losing our children comes out in all shapes and sizes. My guilt is that I didn't wake up in the middle of the night, sensing something wrong. Knowing what I know now about SIDS I understand that even if I had been there with him I wouldn't have been able to save him. That knowledge doesn't make me *not* wonder "what if" though.

Those who lost their infants when they were with other people have other kinds of guilt. What if they hadn't sent them to daycare? What if they had kept their baby home that day? What if they had reminded the daycare owner one last time not to put their baby to sleep on their tummy?

There is a very, very small part of me that thinks that had I been the one up with Toby he wouldn't have died. My very presence would have somehow saved him. I think other mothers feel like if they had been with their babies that day they would also still be alive. I don't think any amount of logic can ever truly make us feel any differently in our hearts. That's just the way we're wired.

Jen's experience

My son died at daycare. He was fine the night before and that morning. I dropped him off and he was happy, smiling. Something made me linger longer than I usually did. I didn't want to let him go. All day at work I thought about him and a couple of times I almost called to check on him. I don't know why. When I got off work I was driving to the daycare when an ambulance sped past me. I got that feeling in my gut like something was wrong. That ambulance could have been coming from anywhere but I knew it had to be something to do with my son. I drove on to the daycare and as soon as I got out of the car the owner met me at the door, crying. He hadn't woken up from his nap. They had checked on him and fifteen minutes later checked on him again and he wasn't breathing. When I got to the hospital he was already gone. He had been gone since he left the daycare. I never got to say goodbye.

When it's not SIDS

Sometimes, an infant's death is prematurely labeled as SIDS until the complete autopsy can be performed. (SIDS is only used as the final cause of death once everything else has been ruled out. It's a cause of death by exclusion.) As a result, some parents have been shocked when they got back their official death certificate and found something else as the cause of death (COD). One of my friends found out that her baby had died of pneumonia. She didn't even know her child was sick. There was no fever, no congestion, and no reason for her to think that her baby wasn't anything but a healthy, happy little girl.

In a few cases, states are leaning away from using SIDS as a COD and, instead, use things such as "unsafe sleeping conditions." One of my friends fought this and had it removed from the death certificate. (The only thing "unsafe" about her son's sleeping conditions was that it was slightly warm in the room-as in 75 degrees. But he was dressed appropriately and there was no sign of overheating.)

Other friends have discovered that their infant had a rare genetic disorder that caused liver problems or heart problems. Even though they had no cause to suspect this and their child showed no signs of being ill, they still feel guilty. After all, as a parent shouldn't you just know by instinct when something is wrong with your child?

And then there are others who watched their children suffer through illnesses that took them suddenly, and sometimes not so suddenly.

There is no "good" cause of death. I don't believe that there is one that gives any kind of comfort over another. I am not happy with my SIDS COD. It means nothing. It means that my child died without any explanation. No matter what it says on that official document, it's just another stab in the heart.

Angel's experience

Our daughter's death was originally labeled SIDS. She was found on her back in her crib with her pacifier and with the fan on. She was swaddled and we didn't use crib bumpers because we were afraid of all the warnings. I put her down at her regular bedtime and I checked on her once during the night. The next morning when I woke up it felt late. I looked at the clock and was surprised that she had slept through her morning feeding. She was blue when I got to her. The coroner told me it was going to be labeled SIDS, probably. Four months later I finally got the death certificate. It was pneumonia. I was so ashamed.

24

How did I not know that my baby was sick? Shouldn't a mother know that? But she had never had a fever, never coughed, never even had a runny nose. I had joined a SIDS forum and apologized to everyone. I felt like an imposter. They had done nothing wrong to lose their babies but I had obviously done something wrong. It took me a long time to learn that it wasn't my fault.

Telling Everyone

Telling people that your child has died is almost certainly the most gut wrenching thing you will ever do. Unfortunately, it never ends. You will, in one form or another, continue to tell people for the rest of your life. Telling them as soon as it happens, though, is the first surreal and painful thing you will probably deal with after losing your infant.

Some people have friends and family who take this chore over for the parents. Bless 'em. Others don't have those folks around or simply want to do it themselves. How *do* you tell people that your baby has died?

My experience

I didn't plan on telling anyone that my child had died. This isn't something that you cognitively *plan*. When I woke up the morning that Toby died, I intended to get everyone dressed, load us all up in the car, and enjoy my day out of the house. Instead, I found myself sitting in a hospital waiting room with a cell phone in my hand, trying to figure out who to call and what to say.

The first phone call was the hardest. I called our best family friend. My words were brief: "Ashley, Toby died. I need you to come to the hospital." He didn't ask any questions. I am sure he was as shocked as I was.

The next call was awful. I called my friend Karen, not knowing that my mother had already talked to her. She was sobbing when she answered the phone. "I'm on my way," she cried.

Next, I called my husband's family. When I told my husband he was not happy about it. "You told them?" he asked. "They're going to find out eventually," I answered. I understood what he meant, though. Telling them made it real. Now that it had been sent out into the universe, the fact that our son was dead couldn't escape us.

Thanks to the advent of mass text messaging and social media, alerting everyone else was far easier than it has been in the past. I am sure people didn't know what to think about my text message: "Toby passed away from cardiac arrest today." Or the Facebook status update that I made as soon as I got home.

To some it might have sounded weird, that I was so ready to get the news out. I *wanted* people to know that he was dead. If I hadn't told them right away then I might not have had the emotional energy to inform them later. I needed to do as much as I could as soon as possible.

This was probably a good thing. In the hospital, I was a veritable machine. I talked to the police, the coroner, the organ donor people, the doctors, the nurses, the well meaning random people in the lobby who had seen his body come in on a stretcher…I had fielded phone calls and texts from friends and signed forms and drawn pictures with Sam.

As soon as I got home I went straight to bed and slept for six hours. I remember nothing else of that day until later when my fiend Becca came over and I showed her the knife that I used to peel potatoes, slightly embarrassed that we had never invested in a potato peeler.

Lucy's experience

My mother made all of the phone calls for me and told everyone. I started calling people but after the first one I just couldn't talk anymore. I wanted to tell them the whole story but I realized that wasn't possible to do over and over again. Later, when people gathered at the house, I wanted to describe every little thing that had happened, down to the last detail. People were uncomfortable. I kept reliving the moment I was told that he was dead. I wanted to relive it because it still didn't seem real.

What do you say?

What do you say when your child has died? How do you say it? Some of the common euphemisms that I have used over the past couple of years include:

He passed away.

My son died.

My son passed on.

My youngest son passed a few years ago.

I lost a child.

Some of the euphemisms I have heard my fellow bereaved parents use include:

He/she went to be with God.

He/she is an angel now.

My child got his/her angel wings.

My son/daughter got called home to Heaven.

No matter how you say it or how nicely you put it, it doesn't change the fact that your child is dead. That's the hard part. I have experimented with different ways of saying it, but they all mean the same thing: He's gone and he isn't coming back. I have yet to find a "nice" way of saying that my son is no longer with me.

Explaining the death

Then, of course, there is explaining the death itself. Infant loss is a tricky one. Infant loss gets grouped in with miscarriage and stillborns, despite the fact that all three are very different things. To be honest, sometimes it makes me mad. Why is infant loss separated from "regular" child loss? Why is there a distinction? I have encountered quite a few people who seem to think that because my child was an infant when he passed away his loss is somehow less significant.

On more than one occasion I have had to explain that my son was not a stillborn. People want to believe that he was. When I say that I have lost a child many people automatically assume that he was lost in-utero. They are surprised to find out that he was two months old when he died and that I was not two months *pregnant*. During one exchange, the woman actually asked me if I had named him before he died.

That aside, however, explaining the death itself is tough. People want to know *why* your child died and how. It's natural curiosity on their part so you can't blame them. Sometimes, though, it feels like they want to know because they are trying to figure out what went wrong. After all, babies don't just die without any reason. They're looking for holes in the story so that they can pick at them to reassure themselves that it won't happen to them.

And sometimes they're just nosy.

Right after Toby died I announced that he had died from cardiac arrest. That's what they were calling it because that's what they call most deaths until they know what they really are. My cousin wrote me and asked if I thought it might be SIDS. At that point, none of us really knew the semantics of SIDS. We didn't yet know that SIDS is not a cause of death but a cause of death by exclusion. Believe me; no parent aspires to have their child's death ruled as SIDS. What it means is that they just don't know.

Along the way I encountered more people who wanted to know other things.

Was he sick before he died?

Was he sleeping with us?

Did he use a pacifier?

Was he a preemie?

Did he overheat?

Were there ANY signs at all?

One well meaning soul, bless her heart, shook her head sadly at the news and said, "Did you forget to put him on his back?"

Well, screw you.

Occasionally I encountered people who really "got it" and these angels in disguise seemed to come out of nowhere. In a small café in Gatlinburg one elderly woman sighed and said, "And you know, with SIDS deaths they just don't know what causes them and there wasn't anything you could do to stop it."

I appreciate those comments, even now.

How much you tell people and what you tell them is up to you. You do not have to give them the private details of your child's death. On the other hand, if you want to give them a blow-by-blow of the autopsy report then that's fine, too. *You* get to choose the information that you share regarding the death of your child. There is no right or wrong way to proceed with this.

I chose to keep a blog. Everyone who knows me, and lots of people who don't know me, know the details of Toby's death. There are pitifully few details.

What I said in my blog entry (spelling errors and all)…" Toby passed away this morning due to cardiac arrest. We are looking at the funeral being held on Tuesday in Campton with the burial either being at Johnston cemetary in Ezel where Nana is burried or else the Hazel Green Cemetary. Thank you for your thoughts and prayers."

What I was *thinking* when I wrote my blog entry…Oh my God, my baby is dead, my baby is dead, my baby is dead.

Me with my boys (and yes, he *is* wearing two different boots)

Minnie's experience

I still haven't learned how to explain my son's death to people. When I say that he died in his sleep they immediately think heart attack or some horrible disease that he was born with. My son was perfect, though, and there was nothing "wrong" with him. He was nine months old when he died and had never had so much as a runny nose. When I tell people that he died of SIDS I sometimes get questioning looks, like they're trying to figure out which one of the "prevention" things I didn't follow. I have done a lot of research on SIDS since his death and met a lot of other parents and I know now that even following all of those things does not guarantee that your child will live. Still, I hate

those probing questions and talking to people who want all the details

about how we found him. I don't mind answering questions about

SIDS but sometimes it just feels like people are accusing me of doing

something wrong without really coming out and saying it.

When the death is accidental

Parents who lose infants to accidents have a different kind of burden of guilt. In some cases, their child has been accidentally suffocated. My heart goes out to these parents who were exceptional mothers and fathers and grieving as much as the rest of us are.

When I find out that someone's child has died due to an accident my instinct is to give these people a hug. We are *all* the best parents that we can possibly be. The only thing we can do is to try to be gentle with ourselves. If your baby's death was accidental and you don't want to talk about it at random then I would suggest that you don't. I think you should do what makes you feel most comfortable. People don't have to know everything. On the other hand, if it makes you feel better to talk about what happened, then do that. Some people will be assholes about it. Others will be understanding. That seems to be the case no matter what the circumstances are.

Jane's experience

I have three children. I did not co-sleep with them. When my youngest son was five months old, though, he was very cranky one night and just would not sleep. I had his crib pulled up next to my bed so that I could rub his back and give him his bottle. In the middle of the night, though, he started crying and crying. I was exhausted and half asleep so I took him out of his crib and placed him on the bed with me. Sometime during the night he rolled over and fell off the bed. When he did, he got caught between the bed rail and the crib. It crushed his esophagus. I didn't even wake up until the next morning. Guilt? Oh yes. I will always feel like I killed my baby. I've had counseling. I know it was an accident. But I will have to live with that for the rest of my life. Nobody could ever take that horror away.

When announcing your child's death

1. You don't have to be the one to do it. Ask anyone else to do it for you if you want to. People are always looking for a way to help. This is pretty helpful.
2. Don't feel like you have to do it right away.
3. On the other hand, if you want to do it right away then go ahead.
4. Don't feel bad if you have to make a public announcement via social media. Yes, some people need to be told individually. But you can't expect to make three hundred phone calls. Sometimes saying it once is the best and most you can do.
5. Say it using whatever expression you want to use.
6. Don't give details if it makes you uncomfortable.
7. Don't talk about *any* of it that makes you uncomfortable.
8. Don't feel like you have to be strong for anyone, whether it's a BFF or the daycare owner. I broke down in tears telling the woman at the checkout counter at our local grocery store. She probably felt uncomfortable. I'm sure she got over it.
9. You're going to miss telling someone. It happens. Apologize for it if you feel bad. Expect that it will probably happen, though.

10. Expect that you might tell the story of your child's death more than once to the same person. That happens, too. We forget who we talk to.

11. Don't feel like you have to answer every call, text, instant message, or comment on your status. It will be too much. Instead, designate someone else to do that if you have to.

12. On the other hand, if it makes you feel better to respond right away then do that. I stayed glued to Facebook for about a week because everyone was writing about my son and I liked talking about him. It was worse when they finally stopped.

13. Expect that people are probably going to cry or get upset when you tell them. Please don't feel like you need to comfort them or play therapist to them. This also happens a lot. It's not your place to make them feel better about your child's death.

14. You're going to hear a lot of religious talk when you tell some people. If those are your beliefs then you might find them comforting. If they're not your beliefs then you might feel frustrated or angry. How you handle that is up to you.

15. People are going to say stupid things. Unfortunately, that's never going to stop. Sometimes you'll say

something back to them and sometimes you'll let it go. It never really gets better.

Toby at his first writer's retreat, listening to our friends play music

Dealing with Authorities

The last thing you want to deal with when your infant dies is someone asking you a lot of questions that you don't know the answers to, or even those you do. Unfortunately, thanks to a lot of misinformation, bad television dramas, and general paranoia parents who lose infants are often looked at with suspicion.

There is a myriad of people you have to deal with after the loss of an infant. Aside from the paramedics, nurses, and doctors who are trying to help, you also get social workers, coroners, state medical examiners, police officers, and other official people. Some have better bedside manners than others.

I have heard horror stories about some of the things that the parents have gone through. Some were treated with so much indignity that they felt like criminals. Others were treated very well, like we were.

My experience

Toby was dead when I discovered him. The paramedics, upon arrival, could have simply called the coroner. There was nothing they could do for my son. Instead, one of them took him in his arms and raced down our stairs and out to the ambulance. They valiantly tried to resuscitate him while I held his breathing tube along the way. I even asked one of them at one point if there was "any hope" and a burly looking guy answered, "There's always hope, honey." Of course, there wasn't.

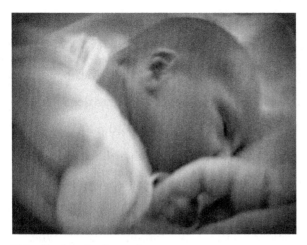
Toby, the day after he was born

Moments after taking him into the examination room the doctor emerged and told me that he was gone. They let me go in immediately. I was alone. My mom and husband had not arrived yet. I went in and there was a nurse in there. She was crying.

We were at the hospital for a very long time since his body had to be moved to the state capital for an official autopsy. Also, our coroner was up on the mountain and it took him several hours to be contacted. During that time we were allowed to stay in the room with him, unsupervised. Friends were also allowed to come in. by the time they took him away his little body was splotchy and blue. Blood occasionally ran from his little nose and I kept trying to clean it with a paper towel.

When the coroner arrived his first statement was, "Bless his little angel heart." He asked us a few questions and then told us that it was probably going to be labeled a SIDS death. Someone else came in and asked me if I wanted to donate his organs. I did. A police officer then accompanied me to a telephone (no idea when he showed up) where I had to spend the next half hour answering health questions like was Toby sexually active and how often did he smoke. I kept breaking down into tears and the officer kept handing me tissues. When I hung up he said, "I don't know why they make you do that," in disgust. He left soon afterwards and we never saw him again.

I didn't speak to any social workers.

Before they took Toby's body away they allowed my mother to hold him one last time.

The coroner came out to our house and looked at the bedroom and took pictures. He also sat with my husband and talked to him for more than an hour. My husband was sure Toby's death was his fault and he was all but confessing to murder. The coroner was patient and assured him he did nothing wrong. The next day he called and left a message on my husband's voicemail and said that suffocation, accidental or otherwise, had been ruled out right away. He wanted him to hear that.

That was the end of the official business for us. Despite everything that would happen later, I couldn't have asked for, or imagined, more patient and kind people than what I encountered.

What they might do

1. Take pictures of the baby's bedroom and sleeping arrangements.
2. Ask you questions about your baby's health leading up to their death.
3. Take any bedding or blankets that were with your child.
4. Question you and your spouse separately.
5. Bring in a social worker to talk to you.
6. Tape record your conversation.
7. Ask for permission to access your pediatrician's records.

Susan's experience

Nothing could have prepared me for the way the authorities acted. My daughter died of SIDS at home and they immediately began treating me like a suspect. They roped off her bedroom and wouldn't let me in it for almost a week. They also took the blanket she was sleeping with (she was ten months old when she died) and never gave it or the clothes that she was wearing back to me. I don't know what happened to them. Although an official investigation was never opened up I always felt like a suspect. A social worker came out to the house a few times and talked to me about "safe sleep." But she died on her back, in a crib, without any stuffed animals or bumper pads in there. I had done everything right.

Organ donation

You might be asked if you want to donate your child's organs. If you do this then you will probably have to answer a lot of medical questions and you'll have to do it right away. It took me about thirty minutes, from what I remember anyway.

Children's organs are used for different reason. They most commonly take the kidneys, heart, eyes, and other small pieces of tissue. It is important to remember that not all donations go to other children. Sometimes they also go to research so be prepared for that as well.

If your child's organs are donated to another child you may or may not ever hear from that family. We didn't. We don't actually know what happened to Toby's organs. You are not allowed to get in contact with the recipients yourself.

It is still possible to have an open casket funeral after organ donation. The infant's body is clothed for burial, so you won't see any visible signs of organ or tissue donation. In skin donation, the sample is taken from the back and it's very thin, like the top layer of a sunburn.

You do not pay anything if you choose to have your child's organs donated. The recipient's family (or insurance company) pays for these costs.

For about a year after his death we continued to receive items from the state organ donor foundation. We got a Christmas tree ornament, Christmas card, and other notes that were actually pretty nice. I am glad that this was a decision we made, even though answering those questions right after his death and trying to focus was difficult.

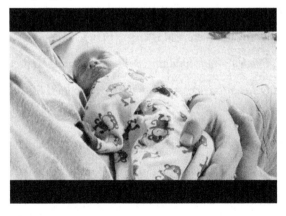

Religion

For many, religion is a place they are able to find comfort in. Their faith helps see them through the toughest parts of their depression and the members of their church act as a support system for them. For others, however, religion is not the comfort that it can be and they might even find that it adds to their anxiety.

Wanda's experience

I was raised a Christian. My parents had me "saved". They made us go to Church some and then we just stopped. I personally believe that there is something out there that is bigger than us, I don't know if that is a "God". I haven't done anything faith-related since Lindsey died except having two preachers speak at her viewing. I feel like any little bit of faith I had has left since she died because I just don't understand how a "god" could just take these babies in the night. Then, I get these signs from Lindsey or ladybug visitors and it really makes me question it. I've seem ghosts too, so that makes me question it. I've also been with several people as they pass away and they all always talk to people

"on the other side", so that makes me question it. So, I guess in short,
I'm faith challenged at the moment.

If it helps

If you find that participating in your religion's rituals, ceremonies, and other acts of worship is helpful to you in your time of grief then, by all means, participate as much as you can. Some churches offer grief support groups that might be helpful and some ministers also work as counselors. Talking to someone you know and trust, rather than a stranger at a doctor's office, might make you more comfortable.

In larger congregations you might be able to find others who have also suffered child loss and connecting with those might provide you with added support. Some grieving parents have even been able to start foundations and charities in their children's names with the help of their church and the support they receive there.

Still, even if your faith is strong don't be surprised if it sometimes falters. It's okay to ask questions, to have lapses of faith, and to wonder if you're even a believer anymore. Everyone goes through this at some point. You have just lost your child and even though you want to put your life in God's hands and believe that he knows what he is doing, it's not always easy to reconcile your loss with this. As your child's parent you believe that the best place in the world for your child was with you.

Amy's experience

I don't know what I would have done without my faith in God. It hurt to lose Aiden but I knew that God had taken him and that he wasn't in pain any longer. Our church was so supportive of us. They had a fundraiser and raised money for his burial expenses. They also organized food and brought it to us for about two months after he died. There were a few times that I wanted to stop believing in God but whenever I would feel like that I would get what I knew was a sign from God and Aiden and that everything was alright.

If it doesn't help

So what about the agnostics and the atheists? Where do they fit in this picture? Many support groups and child loss books are spiritual in nature. If you're a non-believer, or even if you believe in a little bit of everything, things that are too religious might not offer you any comfort and could even make you feel uncomfortable.

There are surprisingly few grief organizations that are secular in nature. Recently, an online support group formed on Facebook called "Grief Beyond Belief." It was created for atheists. Here, you can talk about your loss with other non-believers in an environment that is friendly and supportive. (I joined and I am not even an atheist.) When my friend Karla's son passed away she talked to other mothers who had suffered the same loss but they looked to God for comfort and she couldn't do that. She wondered where the people were who could help her and did not worship an entity that she felt stole her baby from her arms just to have another angel for himself. After all, she felt (like all of us) that her son should still be home with *her* in *her* arms.

There are several ways of dealing with people who try to comfort you with religion. One is to simply be polite and ignore them. As you've probably already figured out, words of comfort are often offered for the person giving them, not the person receiving them. Someone telling you that everything is okay because your child is now with God is probably something that makes them feel better when they are thinking about your child.

If you feel the need to say something back, though, then you can.
You can always politely respond that you appreciate the
thoughts but that you don't practice that religion or share those
beliefs.

My experience

I am not a Christian. I don't hold Christian beliefs when it comes
to the afterlife. Although I do believe in a bigger power, I do not
subscribe to the Christian idea of a God. Being from a very
religious area, this has been difficult for me. When Toby died it
became even more difficult since many people in my life wanted
to comfort me with words and thoughts from the Bible. My
reaction depended on their attitude and who they were to me.

I was polite to complete strangers. I didn't feel like it
was the time to get into discussions with them about religion.

I was polite to the older generation because it just felt
wrong not to be.

I was polite to those I didn't see very often.

Occasionally, however, I talked back. If it turned into a
lecture or I became too uncomfortable then I would interrupt
them and explain that I didn't share those beliefs but that I

would be happy to have a conversation about my own beliefs. This often went over like a ton of bricks.

I found that some people were very confused about my beliefs. They thought that since I wasn't Christian I didn't believe in an afterlife or a higher power. I guess they thought that since I wasn't Christian I must be atheist. I grew impatient with those who would tell me that I could believe anything I wanted but that THEY knew that Toby was in Heaven. I didn't like the idea of someone thinking that they knew my son more than me.

Karla's experience

Being an Atheist has actually made me feel quite isolated in my grief for a long time. I felt I had to take on some of the wording, like "angel baby" to almost fit into the clique. Two years after I lost Kyle did I finally found a site "Baby Loss for Agnostic and Atheist Moms." I was so grateful to finally find this Facebook group after years of hearing the clichés of religion tied to baby loss. Although I found many sites helpful I also pulled away from some because they posted thing like "you can only get through this loss by knowing you will see them again". This just made my anger worse when I was/am proof that this was not true. I am getting through without the belief I will see my baby again and I think I'm doing it better than some with that belief. I was lucky to have friends and family around me and their support is what I needed the most but not having anyone to truly relate to on the Facebook sites was depressing at times and made me feel alone in a place I was supposed to feel the exact opposite.

Coming Home

There is nothing like coming home from the hospital, after being told your infant is dead, and having to face an empty house and their bedroom. It is the saddest, loneliest feeling in the world. There is no well on this earth that is deep enough to convey the hollow feeling that you feel inside. And hollow is about the only word to describe it. The quietness is overwhelming. I remember our house being full of people and it still felt so quiet since there wasn't a baby's cry anywhere.

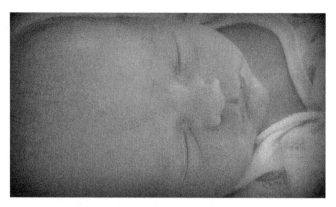

Toby, napping at his first picnic

My experience

I remember coming home from the hospital. I walked straight through the house and the first thing I noticed was that his swing was missing from the living room. My mom noticed that I noticed. "Ashley and I put it up so that you wouldn't have to see it," she said. I went upstairs, ate a bowl of soup in bed, and promptly fell asleep.

At some point, it could have been that day or a week later, my friend was doing my laundry. She asked me if I wanted her to wash his dirty clothes. I freaked out. She understood. For almost six months we left his dirty clothes in his hamper in the same corner of the room that it was in when he died. I couldn't do anything with them so I eventually put them in plastic bags with zippers and stored them in a chest. I am sure they still smell like him and are covered in spit up. I will never wash them.

I had no idea what to do with his stuff. Everything made it look like he was coming back to it. His car seat was still in the car. His stroller had a little diaper in the seat. His pacifier was in his cradle. His lotions and powders were open on his changing table. The box of wipes was half used. There was still a lot of formula left in his last can. It was like he had simply vanished.

I took to sleeping with one of his little outfits that still had spit up on it. I slept with it curled in my hand. Sometimes I drug my sleeping bag into his room and slept on the floor with a candle lit. I cried myself to sleep every night and often woke myself up crying.

Eventually, I was able to pack up a lot of his things. The things that he had worn I kept in a trunk. The things that he hadn't worn but still had the tags on them I tried to give away to people who were having babies. (There were a lot.) Some took them readily. Others didn't seem to care and this hurt my feelings. I felt like they were rejecting Toby.

During those first few weeks, however, my arms had never felt more useless or empty. I had spent the past two months holding him almost every minute. Suddenly, with his weight gone, I literally felt as though a body part had been removed. I often found myself rolling up a pillow and cradling it. I balled up my soft bathrobe and held onto it. Hugging my surviving son helped, but it wasn't the same. I missed and needed the weight of a baby.

Things I did when I got home

1. Updated my Facebook status.
2. Wrote a quick blog entry informing everyone what had happened.
3. Stripped down and went to bed.
4. Ate a bowl of soup.
5. Rearranged the towel closet in the guest bathroom.
6. Stored some extra pieces of luggage in the attic.
7. Changed the sheets on my other son's bed.
8. Ate dinner.
9. Took a bath.
10. Watched Lifetime.

None of those are in any particular order.

People told me to take it easy on myself. Friends came over and helped. Someone started scrubbing my toilets. Someone else did my laundry. Another person offered to get rid of my feral cats. When my phone started ringing and I went into the whole spiel about how he had died (no idea who that was that called) a friend gently told me that I didn't have to do that. I wanted to.

In fact, the only thing I wanted to do was talk about his death and clean. I alternated between the two. I described how I found him to found him to anyone who would listen. In between those conversations I separated laundry and rearranged towels. I'm a stress cleaner. Really, those days are kind of blurry but weird things do jump out at me. I know that a lot of people came over. I can remember my husband's co-worker fixing me some soup and being surprised that I ate it. I remember someone else making some phone calls for me. I also remember my cousins, the ones who never visit, coming over and sitting on the couch with me while I watched TV. As I sat there and my male cousin patted me on the shoulder I couldn't help but think to myself, "So this is what it takes to get everyone here."

At night, when I went to bed, it felt surreal that I would not be up feeding my baby. There was no way I could sleep through the night when I had been used to staying up and feeding Toby. I took some Tylenol PMs. They helped. I also clung to my other son and couldn't stand the thought of him sleeping alone in the other room.

Things you might feel right away

1. Depressed.
2. Empty.
3. Sad.
4. Angry.
5. Like crying all the time and not stopping.
6. Unable to concentrate on anything or remember anything.
7. Forgetfulness.
8. "What if"s
9. Guilt.
10. That you're going crazy.
11. Physical exhaustion.
12. Extreme hunger or lack of appetite.
13. Trouble breathing.
14. Anxiety.
15. Overprotective toward spouse or surviving children.
16. The need to talk about your child and relive their death.

17. Your child's presence.
18. Isolated even in crowds.
19. Feelings that others around you aren't taking the loss as hard as you.
20. Feeling like you're doing well, only to suddenly start feeling awful again.

Jane's experience

When I came home from the hospital the first thing I wanted to do was scrub my toilet. I know it sounds weird but my mom had told me that people would want to come over and pay their condolences and all I could think of were the pee stains that might be around the rims. So, as soon as I walked in the house I started scrubbing at them. I did that to every toilet in the house. I bleached them, scrubbed them...you could have eaten off my toilets. Then I made my husband go out and rent some stupid zombie movie from the video store and I watched it in bed. I fell asleep and never knew that we had visitors.

The Funeral and Burial

Nobody ever intends on planning their child's funeral. You might get life insurance policies for them but you don't *really* plan on your child dying before you.

My experience

On the afternoon of his death my mom came into my bedroom and started asking me questions about the funeral and burial arrangements. There was no question as to where he would be buried-we would put him next to my grandmother in what has kind of become our family cemetery. Did I want our family friend to sing? Sure. Normally I wouldn't have asked such a thing of a man I only saw once a year but suddenly it didn't seem unreasonable. What songs did I want? She suggested "Amazing Grace" but that immediately turned me off. I didn't want what I perceived to be a standard, clichéd religious song. I wanted something special. I remembered playing the Emmylou Harris version of "Green Pastures" on a drive to Bob Evans with Toby in tow. He seemed to like it. I wanted that song. I also wanted Natalie Merchant's version of "When They Ring Those

Golden Bells." Before she left the room I threw out "Silent Night." Yes, it was August.

I picked out an outfit for Toby to be buried in. It was one we had bought him the day before he was born. I had no idea when I was trying to match bibs and shoes that he would one day be buried in it. Later, my mom came back and told me that we needed to find him a hat because during the autopsy they had cut his head open and the wound would show. That conversation sounded as surreal then as it does now.

Melissa, a girl I had last seen fifteen years before in high school, was there with me at the time. We hadn't spoken since we were both teenagers. The first thing I said to her was, "Let's go upstairs. I need to find him a hat."

Toby is buried in Menifee County in Eastern Kentucky. It takes us around 1.5 hours to get there now. At one point my husband's dad said (to me), "I wonder why they buried him way out here..." As though neither one of us had a say in it. The cemetery itself is located on the ridge where my grandparents' farm was. It's only about a mile from that location. There isn't anything built up around it so it's completely isolated and rural. The setting itself is peaceful and beautiful.

The funeral home was run by someone we knew. (In a county the size of the one I am from, everyone kind of knows everyone if you play twenty questions long enough.) They had

59

not done the funeral service of an infant before. They only
charged us their overhead fees. My father-in-law paid for part of
it. It took us almost a year to pay off the rest. It took us nearly
seven months to be able to afford to get a headstone.

The funeral itself was a blur. I read a poem that I had
found on the internet the night before. I talked about Toby and
how he preferred "Who's the Boss" over "Full House." I talked
about how he loved me to sing "The Itsy Bitsy Spider" and act it
out with my hands. It felt important to talk about him and his
personality. It was over quickly. I rode in the hearse with his
body. It was a long drive from the funeral home to the cemetery-
almost an hour. I chatted the whole way. I talk when I get
nervous. It was Toby's last ride. I wanted to point things out to
him along the way. I would never be able to show him the
countryside or my favorite old house again.

We stayed until the gravediggers had finished filling the
grave. When the first clod of dirt hit the casket I wanted to
scream. I sat down on the ground and tried not to look. My
friend sat beside me and sang me old country songs so that I
couldn't hear the rest of the dirt. Once the grave was filled we
decorated it with the flowers.

When I got home from the funeral there were lots of people at my house. I fixed a plate of food, took a few bites, and promptly threw up.

When I say that the cemetery is out in the middle of nowhere, I mean it. There is nothing nearby. As a kid, when I would go to visit Nana's grave I would inevitably have to pee as soon as I got there. On the far side of the property, there is a large tree. (Don't worry, it's in the forest-there aren't any graves anywhere near it.) I'd have to go behind it. Now, Sam almost always has to go when we get there so he uses the tree. That tree has seen pee from at least two generations. I hope that's not my legacy.

Planning the funeral and burial

My mother did all of the planning for me, with me just giving her my input as to what I wanted done. Because Toby was an infant his body had to be sent to the state coroner's office for an official autopsy. Someone came and collected his body straight from the hospital. The funeral home that we contacted then arranged to have his body brought to the funeral home.

The funeral home will normally take care of the paperwork such as filing the death notice and death certificate and arranging burial with the cemetery. You can use a funeral home while still going with cremation.

If you have to wait for an official autopsy, like we did, the funeral might be several days after the actual death. This can be a good and bad thing. I was ready for the funeral by the time it came. The funeral, though awful, offered a little bit of finality. Waiting in the days leading up to it were horrible because Toby wasn't at home with us and he wasn't at the funeral home. I didn't know where he was, for the first time since he had been conceived. Leaving him in the funeral home after visitation and before the funeral was equally awful. I felt like I was abandoning my baby.

This is one time when relying on friends and family to help out is something that you really shouldn't pass up if you get the opportunity. People tend to disappear a bit afterwards but most are more than happy to help around the time of the burial. Karla Roy had people cook meals and drop them off both before and after the funeral and her mother took her older son for a few nights so that she and her husband could have some alone time to "grieve and yell and not have to put on a front for him." Friends and family also helped get the tribute and cards done for her.

Toby's grave

Valerie's experience

From what I can remember, we were in a complete fog and our families helped us plan just about everything. There was even a point where my

husband's family (where we were staying since the day we lost Haylie)
was downstairs trying to word an obituary for her. I remember not
liking that and going down and telling them that Mitch and I could
write it on our own. I guess I just wanted it to be special from us. So
anyway, Mitch and I went back upstairs and tried our hardest but just
couldn't do it. Reluctantly, we went back down and asked for help. We
just answered yes or no to all of their ideas. Everything turned out
beautiful for her, but I do wish that we would have been capable of
planning some of the details ourselves. I would have definitely shopped
around for a different mortuary. I found them to be a little bit tacky
after the dust settled. A couple of weeks later, they mailed us a survey
on how their services were. I ignored it and shortly after, they sent
another one. I did their stupid little survey then, but with the way I've
become from all of this now, I think I'd call and cuss them out for being
insensitive.

Things I did

1. Got a clipping of his hair.
2. Took pictures of him in his casket.
3. Buried him with my "Mom" locket.
4. Kissed him and held his hand in his casket.

5. Took pictures of the pallbearers carrying him to the hearse.

6. Chose songs I actually liked for the service.

7. Read a poem.

8. Stayed until he was in the ground and covered.

9. Picked flowers from our yard to put in the grave with him.

10. Told him I loved him.

Things I wish I had done

1. Pulled up a chair next to his casket and sat there during his visitation.

2. Had someone take pictures at the visitation. (I can't remember who all was there.)

3. Had someone make out thank you cards to those who provided food and other things during the visitation.

4. Had someone videotape the funeral. The only person I know who filmed a little bit of it never spoke to us again or offered to send us the tape.

5. Designated someone to keep track of who was there, who brought which flowers, who sent cards, etc.

Karla's experience

One of the things I remember most was wandering around the shopping mall going into every store and getting so damn frustrated that I couldn't find a little suit for Derek to wear and was getting more and more upset that I even had to be looking for a little suit for Derek to wear to his brother's funeral. My sister-in-law called me just at that moment and could hear the sorrow and distress in my voice. She told me to go home and that she was going to take care of it. It was a tremendous relief. I didn't even realize how much, If she would have just asked me if she could help, I probably would have said I'm already here and I'll find something and then gotten worse, but she just out right told me that she would get it.

Things to do if having a burial

1. Choose a burial outfit. (One they wore, one they didn't get to wear, a brand new outfit, the "coming home" outfit…) If you're choosing one that was special then remember that you won't be able to make a shadowbox with it or frame it or anything later. Sometimes I wish I

hadn't buried Toby with the blanket I did. I wanted him to have it, but sometimes I miss seeing it.

2. Choose the cemetery. Some people want one that is close. Others want one that is special to them. Don't let anyone else influence your decision.

3. Find out if there are any rules about flowers at the cemetery. Some only allow live ones. Others don't mind what you leave. We leave toys and everything on Toby's grave. It looks tacky but we don't care.

4. If you want to be buried near your baby see if you can go ahead and purchase a plot now. At our cemetery we just have to put markers where we want to be buried. We don't have to pay anything until we actually die.

5. Decide if you want a plastic, copper, wood, particle board, or steel casket. You will also have to choose a vault. Our casket was so little that the lid itself was a vault.

6. See if your funeral home has a pricing plan. We paid our costs in installments. They weren't pushy about getting paid.

7. Choose a marker or headstone. You don't have to do this now. It usually takes about six weeks for them to come in. Depending on where you live, you might not be able to have it set until the ground thaws.

Flowers at Toby's funeral

Things to do if cremating

1. Find out if the funeral home cremates infants for free and if they do it onsite or not.

2. Decide if you want your baby present during the services for a final viewing. A sample casket is usually available for this.

3. Decide on an urn.

4. If you don't choose an urn first then the funeral home will usually give you the ashes in a thick, plastic container. Be prepared for this.

5. Also be prepared for the fact that infant ashes are very small.

6. You don't have to decide right away what to do with the ashes. Some people keep them. Others spread them. Some do both.

7. Ask if your baby can be cremated with a special blanket or clothing.

My mom's high school graduating class made this for the funeral.

Things to do if you're having a service:

1. Decide if you want the service to be in a funeral home, church, or other location. Some people only have graveside services. Some have both.

2. Decide on any special music.

3. Gather photos and any other mementos that you might want displayed at visitation and the service.

4. Have someone prepare a slideshow or make one yourself. (I made one myself. Others might want to ask

someone else to do it. Ask the funeral home if there is a way to show it. We set up a laptop by the casket.)

5. Decide if you want an open or closed casket.

6. Pick any special poems or stories that you might want read. You can read these yourself, have the preacher read them, or ask friends and family.

7. Decide who you want to officiate the service. You can ask a preacher you know, ask the funeral home to find someone, or not use a preacher at all.

8. Decide on the kind of service you want and convey that to the officiator. We chose not to go with a highly religious service. Our preacher was fine with this. Others want actual preaching. This is okay as well. It's up to YOU.

9. Ask the funeral home if they provide programs.

Toby's casket

Other things to keep in mind

1. Ask the funeral director anything you want. This is no time to be shy.
2. Don't be afraid to ask for help. My mom got criticized for seemingly "taking over" the planning of the funeral. I was glad she did. I just wanted to choose the music and stuff and show up.
3. You don't have to wear black. And you have the right to request that others don't.
4. Don't feel bad about asking people not to bring their children. Or, if you don't mind the little ones, consider having a "baby room" or "play room" and someone in there watching them during the service.
5. Ask someone to take pictures of the service and visitation. If you don't want pictures of your baby's body then tell them this.
6. Don't be afraid to have a traditional service or something unique. This is your baby's service. Do what makes you feel happy and comfortable.

7. Don't be afraid to have a non-religious service. If you don't want religious songs or scriptures read then convey this.

8. Don't be afraid to have a religious service. There might be people who come who are opposed to this but this isn't about them.

9. You can follow religious traditions that are important to you but also create new ones as well.

10. Ask the funeral home if you can hold your baby one last time if you want to.

11. There is no right or wrong way to plan a service.

12. You don't have to have a service with your baby's body present. You can have a private burial and then hold a memorial service later if you wish.

13. Don't let anyone pressure you or rush you into making decisions.

14. You might also like to have a balloon release as part of a graveside service. Don't be afraid to do things that others might deem as being "fun."

15. Don't be afraid to include your other children. Some people think that children do not belong at funerals. If you are okay with this and want to include your surviving children, and they want to participate by singing or reading a poem, then let them.

16. Don't feel obligated to play a traditional song. I had "Silent Night" sung. It was August. Others have had lullabies or even popular music. It can be pre-recorded, live, or audience participation.
17. Some people also read children's books at services.

Toby's casket was so small it almost got dwarfed by the flowers

Wanda's experience

I wish we would have researched funeral homes in the area a little more. We ended up going with the one the Sheriff recommended in town. Well when we got to her service, half of the funeral home had been in a fire recently. And then, to have her cremated they didn't do that on site, her body had to travel an hour away. I refrained from using the good funeral home that I knew about because my dad works for that owner and sometimes at the home and I thought it'd be hard for him. [My husband] and I planned it all. Once her body got to the funeral home from the M.E. office we went in and picked everything. I remember it well. They kept asking us this and that and we didn't know how to respond. We obviously had never planned before and were completely lost. We had two preachers form a church come and bless her and say several things from the bible, which we left up to them. No clue what they said, I don't remember. I decided on no pictures and I'm still feeling that way. We had a viewing of her lying in the casket a day and a half after she died. Then she sat in the freezer for over a week before they took her down for cremation. We didn't embalm her and she was cremated in her outfit with her ladybug "lovie", purple frog wubbanub, and the receiving blanket she came home from the hospital in. I should mention, we didn't pay a dime. B/c she was an infant they said we didn't have to worry about the cost. Her urn is with all of her ladybug collections and pictures on our mantle......we want to find a place for her but haven't found the shelves or cabinet we are looking for yet. I'll know it when I see it.

Finding Support

Finding support is really, really important but it is hard since it often feels like nobody wants to listen to you talk about your child and those who do get worn out quickly in what I like to call "friend fatigue." So who can you talk to? There are the obvious ones like counselors and support groups but online support systems are becoming really popular as well. I have joined them all.

Fellow grieving mother, Wanda, made this for me and posted it on Toby's birthday

Melissa's experience

About two months after losing Scooter I found that my grief did not seem to be lessening at all. I did join an online support group which made me feel like I was not alone. Watching new members come along almost weekly as a result of infant loss (SIDS) was difficult. I wanted to meet someone in person who is going through this so I went to a Perinatal Loss support group at Dayton Children's Medical Center. I did meet a couple there who lost their child to SIDS. It was heartbreaking to hear their story but helped me to be in their company. After a couple of meetings I did not feel any relief and have just basically given up on the idea of "healing" as so many like to put it. 2-1/2 years into this and the waves just knock me down at times. I have several friendships with mothers of these sweet little ones that I hope will continue for a long time to come. It has helped me so much to see them having their rainbows and gives me some faith that life does go on and that happiness truly can come to you over time.

Support groups

People started talking about support groups almost as soon as

Toby died. My friend Heather talked me into going to my first

support group. Well, she didn't talk me into it so much as she

wrote me and told me we were going. I was cool with that. It

was a small meeting with just a handful of us but I think that's

better, at least at first. They were all parents who had lost

children, but none of their children had been infants so we were

kind of on different wavelengths. Still, there were some

commonalities and it was good to talk to people who have "been there."

What surprised me the most was that although mine was the most recent, with the other losses having happened years ago, it was still so fresh for everyone. That's what I hate about putting a deadline on grief. You never really "get over" it. You just can't. Things get a little easier and you don't find yourself breaking down and bawling in the middle of Wal-Mart as often, but it's still there.

We also talked about "things people say" to be "helpful" and we all laughed because we have all heard the same things. My favorite at the time was, "He's in a better place." Well, I don't want him in a better place. I want him right here, in this *crappy* place, with me. Or the Pizza Hut waitress who told us that it was okay because he was with Pete's Mom. (We even got bits of this before she died.) Hey, what's wrong with my dead relatives?

Anyway, that's some of the crazy stuff that goes through your head sometimes.

When I started talking about his funeral, though, they couldn't believe that the gravediggers started filling in the hole while we were still there. As my friend said, they were all over that like a worm. It made me uncomfortable. They just wouldn't let it go. When the meeting was over Heather told me she was proud of me for talking. The moderator, though, told me that I might be more comfortable in an infant loss support group.

So, I went to one of those next.

That meeting, however, was full of people who had lost pregnancies since they group pregnancy and infant loss together. So one group had never known their babies outside of the womb and the other had lost much older children, some even adults. I felt like I didn't have a place. I even felt awkward in the pregnancy loss group because I felt guilty since I had gotten to know my baby and play with him. (To be fair, I made some friends in that group and we still keep in touch online.)

Neither group felt right for me.

Grieving parents have different experiences with support groups. Some have found them extremely helpful. Others have gone to them and had a hard time dealing with the fact that many of the parents seem in really bad shape, even though it's been years since their child died. They have gone looking for hope that things will get better and have walked away feeling like nothing ever will. On the other hand, other parents have had the exact opposite effect: they've gone to the meetings and seen people dealing with their child's death in healthy ways and they've left feeling a lot better and very hopeful.

The dead kid club

About six months into my grief I started exploring online
communities after my "real world" grief support groups didn't
help me in the way I hoped they would. After some hits and
misses, I finally found "my people." These were crazy, grieving,
angry and bitter people just like myself. I loved them. (They are
also incredibly funny, sweet, and caring individuals and I credit
them with saving my life.) We have since moved over to
Facebook together and after nearly three years of "hanging out"
online we have exchanged phone numbers, email addresses, and
street addresses.

In the beginning, it was our deceased children that
brought us together. Most of us were in the early stages of grief.
After awhile, though, things seemed to change. These days,
although we do talk about our deceased children, they're no
longer the sole foundation of our friendships. These people
(mostly women) know all about Sam and Iris. They send them
presents in the mail, they keep up with their doctors'
appointments, they remember their birthdays...And I do the
same for their living children.

When we're feeling low, we write each other for support. You can also catch us up at 2:00 am talking about mortgages, vodka, foreclosures, surgeries, and men. We have formed a semi fan club for Darryl Dixon and his dirty poncho and relish discussing the latest developments on *The Walking Dead* and *Dancing with the Stars*. We might not always agree on politics or Kenny Chesney but we actually have fun together.

And you should have seen our conversation about historical porn and James Patterson.

I never thought that when I met these people one day we would *not* be spending the majority of our time depressed and crying to each other. If someone had told me that we would eventually be sharing jokes and laughing and making fun of reality television then you might as well have been telling me that I had just won some ocean front property in Arizona.

There are still some days that are hard and we meet all birthdays and anniversaries together. But I really feel like we share more than that. I don't like belonging to the Dead Kid Club but, if I have to, then I am glad that I found friends that make it a little easier.

Online support groups can offer a wonderful way to connect with other parents who have lost infants. There are some that are religious in nature and some that are non-denominational. You can find groups specifically for SIDS, stillbirths, miscarriage, and general child loss. Some communities are more active than others.

I would encourage anyone thinking about signing up for an account to lurk around for a little while, read what the other posters are saying, and get to know the site before you sign up and start baring your soul. Also, look at the last date that anyone posted anything. An active forum is the best one since it means there will always be someone around to talk to.

Many people sign up using fake names and non-identifying information. This may or may not be what you want to do. If you think that you're going to be talking about your friends in real life, any depression, or anything that you don't want the majority of people in your life to know about then creating a pseudo-name for the public forum is helpful.

Things I have encountered on public forums

Mostly, I have had positive experiences on SIDS forums. I have connected with good people and found support and friends. I have run into some really awful people, though, and occasionally the anxiety they cause almost isn't worth the amount of support I find in the group.

There does seem to be a trend that is disconcerting and extremely unhelpful in most cases. I think I can break it down into four categories:

1. "I almost lost my daughter to SIDS"
Scenario: A person comes on and claims that their child "almost" died of SIDS but thankfully lived.

Why it's bad: Aside from the fact that it's impossible (the very name SIDS means "death"-they are probably referring to what they use to call "near SIDS" but now call ALTEs) it's rude. Don't tell a bunch of parents who *did* lose their children that yours "escaped" death. We don't want to hear it. It makes us feel more guilty-like you did something right and we didn't.

2. "SIDS isn't real"
Scenario: Someone comes on and tells us that SIDS isn't real, for

whatever reason. That's it's really suffocation or some really rare disorder that the doctors didn't catch.

Why it's bad: Telling a bunch of parents whose child died from a syndrome that the syndrome isn't even real?

3. "I haven't lost a child to SIDS but I know someone who did so now I am here to tell you all what you did wrong..."

Scenario: An aunt, uncle, friend...whatever comes on and starts telling everyone that *they* didn't lose a child but know someone who did and now they have all the answers. They then start giving us stats, start talking preventive methods, and generally start lecturing us.

Why it's bad: Preaching to the choir. Most of us know more than the medical professionals do at this point. Don't join a forum and automatically assume you know more, especially if it's your first post.

4. "I WON'T lose a child to SIDS because..."

Scenario: A person joins a group and starts claiming that they've never lost a baby and won't because they have bought a Halo sleeper, use the specially wrapped mattresses from New Zealand, walked backwards three times down a flight of stairs...whatever.

Why it's bad: No products have been proven to reduce the risk of SIDS. Plus, it's mean it tell other parents who have suffered a loss that you are above it.

Sometimes, a forum can be helpful. Other times, not so much. I am learning to laugh when I can.

Ellen's experience

It took me awhile to find the support group that was right for me. I ended up trying out a bunch of different ones in my city but I just didn't "click" with anyone there. Nobody else had lost an infant. The people in my support group had all had miscarriages and I just

couldn't relate to that at the time. I wanted to meet someone who had

an experience that was similar to mine.

I did end up joining an online support group and found a lot

of help there. Sometimes the posts would get really religious and I

wasn't into that. If I was having a bad day, having someone get on

there and tell me to "leave it in God's hands" didn't make me feel better

at all. (I am atheist.) But, I made some friends online and I knew that

no matter what time of day it was I would be able to have someone to

talk to. Since I didn't have friends offline I felt comfortable talking

about my feelings to I really think that the online group was my

lifesaver.

Unusual places

Most of the time, it feels like people just don't "get it." And why
should they, really? I mean, I may have lost a child but I don't
understand the pain that someone who lost a spouse might feel.
(Although I think that losing a child might give me a certain
amount of empathy and I have always been able to sympathize.)
Sometimes, though, I find that support comes from the
strangest of places.

Recently, I was getting my hair done and my hairdresser started talking to me about Toby. He told me that his aunt had lost a baby to SIDS forty years ago. We talked about this at length and he totally "got" it. There was no need to explain myself, apologize for not being the same person, or even really say anything at all. He told me that his aunt had never really "moved on" and that, lo and behold, nobody expected her to. His family just took it for granted that she would always be grieving and she would always be a little sad. Interestingly, though, was the fact that she said that in her mind her son continued to age. She saw his first day of school, his high school dances, his graduation, his marriage, her grandkids...all of those "memories" played out in her mind as though they actually happened. That's how she dealt with her grief.

My hairdresser, who has no children of his own, did not think this was strange.

There is a woman whom I only met one time and at that time it was just for a few hours at a one day writing retreat. I don't know this woman and we only talked briefly. However, when Toby died she attended his funeral and then wrote me a beautiful letter afterwards. She has continued to send me random letters and emails over the course of the past year, somehow always knowing the right thing to say.

87

I don't expect to find this support when I am out and about, but it's always a welcomed thing when I do. It takes me by surprise and I am thankful for it.

You might be disappointed by the way that the people closest to you in life are handling your grief but sometimes you do find support in unusual places and from people you weren't expecting to find it from. Opening yourself up about your loss and experiences can be a double-edged knife; on one hand you're letting some of the crazies in and on the other you're also opening up the possibility of connecting with someone who really tries to understand how you feel.

Explaining the pain

I don't regret anything I did in the days, weeks, and months following Toby's death. I don't regret anything I said or did and, if I went back, I would do it again. I'm not sorry for fighting back when my family was attacked and I'm not sorry for not letting things go when people continued to push my buttons.

If I could change something, though, it would be this: I would not waste my time explaining my pain to people.

That doesn't mean that I wouldn't talk about my pain and write about it here-I'd just stop trying to explain it to people in hopes that they would be more compassionate. For that first year, I dedicated a lot of blog entries to explaining my pain and why I was hurting so badly. It didn't stop in my blog, though, because I had to do it in "real life", too. The people who just didn't understand why we didn't move on, why we were still sad or angry, why our world was falling apart...I spent a lot of time talking to these people. I tried to explain a mother's love, how horrible it was to wake up and find your baby dead, the guilt, the sadness, the overwhelming urge to not want to live anymore...I did my best to put all of these things into words for these people so that they could understand and stop being so hurtful.

I wouldn't do that again.

Here's what I have learned: those that "get it", get it; those that don't, won't.

I used to think that one day, when some of these people grow up, get married, and have families of their own they might look back at what we went through and maybe have some semblance of understanding. Maybe then they'll understand that this thing that happened to us is indescribable and horrible and they'll know that they should have been a little easier on us.

I no longer believe that.

Even if those people had their own babies and, God forbid, lost theirs, they'd probably still look back on us and judge.

My energy was completely wasted on these folks. I am sorry for that. I wish I'd figured out a lot sooner that spending so much energy trying to explain to them a pain that they either had no concern really trying to understand or never would anyway was a lost cause because I might have devoted it to something else.

I'm not sorry about writing my feelings down in my blog. That's been helpful. I'm not sorry for having those feelings. I'm just sorry that so much of my time seemed to have been spent educating people as to why I was sad and upset.

Minnie's experience

I got so tired of the people who would say things to me like, "Are you still upset?" Well, hell, of course I'm still upset! These were usually the people who would cry about break ups for years and yet they thought that I should be okay after a few months? That infuriated me. I was so happy when I went to a support group meeting at our local Hospice and met people who had lost other children. Some of them had lost children years and years before and they were still grieving. Thank

God! I didn't feel so bad that I was still in acute pain after only five months. Someone there told me that the "real" pain hadn't even started yet and that I needed to lower my own expectations. That made me feel good. I didn't feel as crazy.

Grief junkies

And just when you think that nobody is being supportive of you, someone comes along who totally gets it and is there for you every second of the day. They're awesome! They're fabulous! They're...starting to get a little creepy.

Grief junkies. Someone threw this term out to me and it stuck. Grief junkies. I knew what they meant as soon as I read it. Grief junkies are the opposite of those people who don't want to talk about your grief with you-these are the people who seem to be all over it.

At first thought you might think, okay, what's so wrong with that? I want to talk about my child and my grief. In the beginning, it might be okay. You meet with these people, usually friends, and they listen attentively while you discuss your feelings, frustrations, and memories of your child. Later, however, things get weird.

They won't let it *go*.

These are people who, even when you're talking about another subject, bring it back around to how awful you're feeling. They bring up your depression, sadness, and grief even when you're not talking about it yourself. They want to know intimate details about how you feel. They want play-by-plays. Then, they start getting even more inquisitive about other parts of your life. They seem to want to play therapist to you.

Most of all, they provoke you. You might be holding it together pretty well, and then the grief junkie will come along and poke and prod at you until you're an absolute mess and they *have* to comfort you. That's kind of how they get off.

There are other examples of this, too. They want to take on your grief as their own. Maybe part of it is to feel empathy, but a lot of it is for attention. They never met your child, or only met them once, yet they talk about how much they are grieving and how much they miss him. They tell other people that they have lost someone close to SIDS-never revealing that it wasn't them at all but someone they knew.

Personal information and feelings that you revealed to them in what you thought were private moments are suddenly showing up in their status updates and blogs. They comment on your own page, revealing that same information-stuff you didn't want made public. They like to show off how much they know about you and your situation.

If you've encountered a person like this then you know what I'm talking about. They're almost worst than the ones who don't care at all.

Angel's experience

There was a woman in my life after I lost my child. I will call her "Judy." Judy was really helpful at first but after awhile it seemed like she wanted me to be upset. I remember once I was having a pretty good day and she kept bringing up my child to me and asking me if I was okay. By the end of the day, I wasn't, but it was thanks to all of her prodding. I mean, I was glad that she was talking to me about him but the timing was totally inappropriate. She would also help out a lot but as soon as she would leave my house she would get on Facebook and brag to her friends about everything she had done for us. Once she even wrote about how I was feeling suicidal. Gee, thanks for broadcasting that to the world!

Trying to support

The phrase "well meaning people" gets thrown around a lot.
When someone says something that's really insensitive and kind
of crappy, other people try to defend them by saying that they
"meant well." There is a difference between people who are just
bad friends and the ones who try to offer support but do it in a
way that is not helpful. Sometimes, the line between the two is
hazy at best.

On a popular grief site there is a list of things that
friends can do to "help" grieving parents. One of these things is
to try to talk them out of making big decisions. I strongly
disagree with this. Sometimes, a big decision that makes no
sense to somebody else is exactly what the grieving parent needs
to do.

For instance, some parents just cannot stay in the home
that they lived in with their infant. The memories are too
painful. Moving is a big decision but really might be the best one
for that family.

Having a subsequent child is another big decision that a
lot of non-grieving parents don't understand. Some parents want
to get pregnant again right away. Most parents I know who
went on to have subsequent pregnancies have said that it's the

best decision they made, although it was a stressful one. (It's a paradox really.)

Early on, when we were talking about getting pregnant again, a friend lectured us on this and tried to talk us out of it. He was wrong. As another one said, "If you want to get pregnant then, as your friends, we should be volunteering to do a naked fertility dance or something. Friends support others, even when they don't understand."

Sometimes, a friend just can't offer the support that you need but they might do what they can. There are people in my life who are terrible listeners but they make excellent casseroles. One of the best things that someone did to us was show up at our house the day of the funeral with lasagna and whiskey.

A month after Toby died the owner or a local B&B invited us to stay for the weekend

Going Back to Work

Thanks to our financial situation, I was unable to take much time off from work. My husband couldn't take any time off. I went back after about two weeks. Luckily, I work from home so I didn't have to deal with getting dressed or anything that might require physical effort. I just had to drag myself to the computer. I did have to deal with demanding clients, though, and some of them didn't cut me any slack.

My experience

One of my best clients sent me $250 as a "bonus" and asked me to take time off. I did. And I appreciated him a lot. We're still together. Another one actually dropped me from the project. He was a little weird anyway.

While working I alternated between wanting to cry all the time and feeling distracted enough by the mundane nature of some of the jobs that I grew kind of numb. I was still measuring things, too. The last time I was in Richmond Toby was alive. The last time I ate spaghetti Toby was alive. This time last week Toby was alive. I couldn't let go of that. I didn't want to. When I thought of him in that way, he still felt close.

One of the reasons I was able to go back to work was because people had been so helpful in those first two weeks. The people that were the most helpful were those that just did things. The ones who wrote or called and asked, "When's a good time for me to come over?" or "Can I see you in a couple of weeks?" or "What can I do?" left me scratching my head. I didn't know how to answer any of those. There was no concept of "a couple of weeks" at that point. I had trouble getting through the hour, much less the day or the week. And as far as doing anything, I wasn't sure what I needed or what I didn't need. My friend came over and painted my toenails green with little polka dots. Apparently I needed that because it made me feel better. Who knew?

Working was easy. It was mindless. That was a good thing because my mind seemed to be going. It occurred to me to feed Sam, but not myself.

While I was able to work, I did become agoraphobic for awhile. Leaving the house even to check the mail seemed to be too big of a hassle. I didn't have a problem getting dressed, getting up, and getting things done but actually stepping outside of the house felt wrong.

For the dad

I was reading this one thing and it said that "dads usually go back to work first because they have to." Like we women are all ladies of leisure or something. Well, my husband went back to work because he had to and because he wanted to. He needed to keep busy. He needed to keep his mind occupied. But, it is true, it seems like men don't get asked how they're doing like the women do. There does seem to be a discrepancy between how society thinks a man should act and how a woman should in regards to working after the loss of a child.

Unfortunately, although my husband was able to return to work things didn't get easier for him. He had two jobs at the time and one of them required him to be there fairly early in the morning. His mind had to be sharp for that job because lots of people depended on him. As depression and anxiety overtook, however, he just wasn't able to perform at the high standards he had been working at. His boss had to let him go a month after Toby died. We understood, and she was very nice about it, but it made things even more difficult for us financially. It meant that we had to take our son out of daycare which meant I had to work full time from home (since we still needed my income to pay most of the bills) and watch a three year old at the same time.

When you go back to work, remember...

1. Grieving is in your heart and your mind. Your job is just another place. The grief will follow you.

2. A lot of people will think that because you're back at work you're "doing better." I say those people can kiss my ass. You might be more polite about it. There are lots of reasons why grieving parents return to work. You don't have to explain your reasons.

3. You don't have to put on a cheery front to make other people feel comfortable. Be nice and polite when you can but don't feel like you have to make those around you feel good in your presence.

4. You'll probably feel like work is pointless. There will be days when you're just going through the motions.

5. You might have trouble getting out of bed some mornings. That's normal. It's *all* normal.

6. If you are getting out of bed, getting dressed, and going to work at all then you are doing fantastic. Don't let anyone else try to convince you otherwise.

7. People will say stupid things to you. You might not always handle that well.

8. You will probably have to take a lot of breaks. Random crying happens. Sometimes you make it to a private place and sometimes you don't.

9. Some people will "deal" with your return by ignoring the fact that you were gone at all. This might make you feel bad. It might also make you feel angry.

10. You might have trouble being around children or other co-workers who have children who are the age of the child you just lost.

11. If you work around kids you might get a lot of questions about what happened.

12. If there is any part of your work duties that you just can't do then talk to your manager or other co-workers. People generally want to help. Let them.

If you're not ready

If you're not ready then you're not ready. Sometimes your financial situation dictates your feelings, though. When you have to work but you feel like you'd rather crawl under a rock and scream than face your co-workers and the general public, then try some of these:

1. Visit your work. Before you go back for a full on day drop in and say "hey." Look around. Sit at your desk. Eat lunch with your co-workers. Dip your toes in a little bit.

2. Ask if you can go back part time for awhile. If you have the kind of job where your hours are flexible this might work until you're ready to table the whole thing again.

3. See if you can telecommute. More and more companies are allowing their employees to work from home. See if yours will.

4. Ask if you can change your office. I know it sounds weird but sometimes a literal change is needed. Move your desk around, get new office furniture…I wanted everything exactly the same. Others don't.

5. Consider finding a job that allows you to work from home. If you just can't go back to your job, see if you can get a job to come to you.

Ellen's experience

I could not go back to work for a long time. I took a year off and then I started working from home. Our family suffered a lot from it. I did try to return to work but on my first day back people were avoiding me and, worse, acting like nothing had happened. It was horrible. There had been a picture up in the coffee room that had my family in it but that had been removed. It was like they were trying to erase us. People acted like I had just been out with the flu or something. Then my boss took me into his office and started lecturing me on how I couldn't "fall apart" because my clients needed me. I was really upset. So, I went back to my desk and wrote out a thirty day written notice, per company policy. I took it to him and he didn't even care. He just shrugged. Then, angry, it told him to never mind-I was giving him my two week verbal notice. I didn't even stay the whole two weeks.

Marriage and Partnerships

My mom says that as she was driving my husband to the hospital one of the first things he said was, "Rebecca will never speak to me again."

Honestly, the thought of leaving my husband and us breaking up did not occur to me. Well, not then anyway. I didn't really want to be around anyone but him and our surviving son, Sam.

Child loss is one of the biggest reasons that couples separate or get divorced. Other than an affair there is no other event in a marriage that could possibly cause as much stress. And I would much rather my husband cheat on me than to have my child die so the affair business is pretty far down on the list for me. There are lots of reasons why a couple might not be able to make it after the loss of a child. The stress alone is enough to cause friction in even the strongest of marriages. And then there is the guilt, the blame (self and otherwise), the depression...

Some marriages actually become stronger, though. Where others find gaps created between them, some couples find themselves closer than ever. I would venture to say, though, that every couple goes through a rough period after the loss of a child. How you pull through it depends on a variety of factors.

Your libido

Many people are shocked to find that after the death of their child they have an increase in their libido. When they think they should be doing nothing but crying and feeling horrible, they suddenly find themselves wanting to be sexually active. There have been studies done on this. Sexual intercourse can be an affirmation of life. I say it probably has something to do with wacky hormones, too.

Dealing with the guilt of a healthy sex drive after the loss of your child can be rough on some people. Having gratification and happiness of any kind is hard to wrap your head around when you are also experiencing the most traumatic and horrible thing that has ever happened and ever will happen to you.

On the other hand, some people don't experience an increase in their sex drive at all. Instead, they might feel a decrease in it and where they once wanted to be physical with their partners on a regular basis, now they can barely stand to be in the same bed with them.

There are also biological and psychological reasons behind this as well. Depression can cause a decrease in sexual appetite. It's another hormonal issue. Even if your mind says it's okay your body might not respond, or vice versa. There can also be psychological factors behind this. You don't want to have sex because you're punishing yourself for not being a better parent, for letting your child die, for not seeing the signs that something was wrong. You want to deny yourself pleasure because your child will never be able to experience anything good again.

What can be particularly hard is when one parent is experiencing an increase and the other is having a decrease in desire. This is more common than not.

Time is usually the "fixer" for these issues. Waiting it out seems to help. Counseling might also be helpful. Antidepressants can help with depression and anxiety but their side effects can also lead to a decrease in desire so they might be counterproductive in this area. It's never good to pressure the other partner into sex just as it's not good to go along with it to please your partner because you might end up feeling angry and this could cause a bigger riff. As with other aspects of your relationship, you shouldn't expect everything to get back to normal quickly. This area of your partnership, like the others, might also take some readjusting to.

Communication

Communication can be so difficult between partners after the death of a child, even if you've always prided yourself on being able to talk about anything. The fact is, everyone grieves differently. That includes you and your partner. Where one of you might be a talker and want to discuss your feelings, the other might not. One of you might feel like "faking it" until you make it and the other might think this is disloyal. One might want to cry in front of others and be emotional and the other wants to keep their feelings to themselves. You can even switch roles after awhile.

If you do feel like you are having a communication breakdown then you might want to try communicating in a different way. I, personally, do NOT recommend getting a friend or family member involved. If you want a mediator then do try to find a professional, neutral one such as a preacher, doctor, or counselor. Other ways that you might try communicating include:

1. Instant message one another.

2. Email each other.

3. Leave each other notes.

4. Text.

5. Leave voicemails for each other.

6. Write in a joint journal or diary.

Yes, these things sound silly and impersonal but sometimes the actual *talking* is the issue. You might find that you're saying things you don't mean in the heat of an argument or that you're not saying anything at all. When you write, however, you have time to think about your words and what you want to say. I actually did this with my husband. It helped.

My experience

The first few weeks after our son died we communicated well with one another. After that, though, things went downhill for us. I wanted to talk about my feelings. He didn't. I wanted to talk about our son. He didn't. He immediately went back to work and stayed up late working. I went to bed alone. We didn't watch movies together nor do anything fun together. I felt abandoned. When I would try to stay up late and talk to him he would lecture me and send me to bed like a child.

We have different beliefs in the afterlife and paranormal. I wanted to talk about these things. He couldn't. My interest in such matters is actually a really big part of who I am but he was completely disinterested in these discussions.

Sometimes, things would get really bad. On more than one occasion my husband suggested that I see a therapist because he couldn't talk to me. I didn't want to talk to a therapist, though. I wanted to talk to *him*. Once, after becoming hysterical, he talked about me going to a hospital. I immediately thought locked-up psych ward. After that I tried not to let him see me emotional. Instead, I blogged more and talked to my friends.

We made the mistake of getting a friend involved. She sat there between us while we had an argument and then tried to play counselor to us by having us say something that we liked about each other. I did it but he wouldn't. It really, really hurt my feelings. It also put her in an awkward position.

My husband is not the greatest at always saying what he means and he took to writing his friends back home about how he was feeling. I thought he should be talking to me about these things. From the things he said, some of them got really bad impressions of me. For instance, even though I organized his trip home to his mother's funeral, when he couldn't go his friends thought I wouldn't "let" him. I read his letters to them and I totally understood why they would think that, after what he had said.

When my husband's family decided to go bat shit crazy on us I had the last straw in my hands. I no longer wanted to be married to him. I just couldn't deal with all of it anymore. I felt abandoned by my husband. When they were saying horrible things about me and calling me names I felt like he should have been defending me. He didn't. Instead, he tried explaining our grief to them, asking them to leave us alone, and ignoring them. None of these things made them stop. I felt like he was feeding me to the wolves by allowing them to treat me the way they were treating me.

The fact is, my husband is not a fighter. His reflex is to shut down and withdraw. This does not always help situations. As a result, I felt like I was left with everything in my lap to contend with: Toby's death, his family's hysterics, even the baby clothes. It was an awful weight on my shoulders.

Luckily, we made it through it. I don't know how. We started emailing one another and this helped. I asked him not to write to his friends, but to talk to me instead. He did. We still have problems sometimes but we work through them. Sexually, things are hit and miss. I also went through an increased libido there for awhile but then some illnesses and surgeries got in the way and we have never really regained that momentum.

Partner fatigue

In most cases, we turn to our partners for our moral and emotional support. It's easy to forget, though, that sometimes they need a break (just like we do). I was reading a blog entry from someone who had lost a child and they talked about how sometimes they were with their partner, enjoying themselves, and then would suddenly break
down into tears and turn the situation into an emotional discussion about their child. I think we can all relate to that. After awhile, though, it does become easier to control it.

There were many times in my own marriage when I felt like an emotional wreck but my husband was having a good

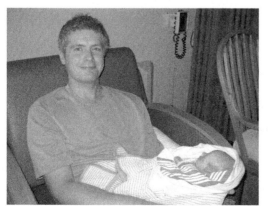

time. I wanted to break down and cry but I knew he *needed* that good time, that good moment, so I held it in. Later, when we got home or something, I gave into the feeling and let it out. But I learned to pick and choose when to do that. It wasn't always easy but it helped his grieving to be able to have some "happy" times here and there. Honestly, it helped me as well.

Going out on Halloween and trying to be normal

Joy's Experience

After our daughter died from the flu at eight months old I really felt like my husband wasn't hurting as bad as I was. He didn't take any time off from work and didn't care what I did with her stuff. He didn't offer to help me pack it up, didn't want to talk about her-he didn't even help with funeral arrangements. I felt like I was completely on my own. He was still interested in sex but I was so angry at him that I couldn't

111

stand to be in the same room with him. He had told me that I was paranoid when she got sick and that she would be "fine." I also held that over his head. I wanted to divorce him and leave him but I couldn't stand the thought of really being on my own. Then, one day, I came home from work early and found him. He had cleaned out his briefcase and was removing one of her little dresses he kept in it. I had no idea that he carried an outfit and one of her old bottles in his briefcase. That changed the way I looked at him. He was grieving, too. Just in a different way. After that we started going to support group meetings together. Things eventually got better but it took more than a year.

A new person

I do think that, along with the death of our child, we also experience our own deaths in a way. I think we become different people. We might even develop new interests, new outlook on life, new goals, and new friendships. These things might not always be compatible with our partners'.

From observation, the couples who have done the best seem to be those who almost start anew in their relationships. I don't feel like we are the couple that we once were. I think we're better in some ways. We have found new things in common, new things we like to do, and new things to talk about. This is good. We were able to take our past and use that as a foundation while still building a brand new relationship.

Kate's experience

My husband and I did not get along well after our daughter died. His parents had never liked me and after she died they blamed me. I was working at the time and she was at daycare. They thought that if I had been a stay at home mom she wouldn't have died. They called me names and said all kinds of horrible things. My husband didn't defend me or stand up for me. He said that he didn't want to "get involved." It was very hurtful because on top my grief I had to deal with that stuff. My husband also wanted to have sex a lot but I was so angry at him and so depressed about our daughter that I just couldn't. I mean, some nights I did anyway just because he was upset and wanted to but I never enjoyed it. We ended up having to go to counseling together. It helped.

Things to remember for your relationship

1. Change is going to happen. Neither one of you is the same person you used to be. But that doesn't mean that you can't try to move forward with what you are now.
2. Everyone grieves differently-even your partner. You can't force them to grieve like you do. But you can try to accept your differences.
3. You might have to change your approach. Since your partner might not grieve in the same way you do, you might have to change the way you approach your partner for awhile. It's hard, but worth it.
4. Try not to blame. Blaming is easy. Everyone does it. But with blame comes resentment.
5. Don't forget to be nice. Saying "thank you" and showing appreciation for the little things that you try to do for one another is helpful.
6. Get out. When you can, get out and do things together as a couple. It might just be a walk, but moving around will help you connect.

7. Don't force. On the other hand, don't force your partner to do something they don't feel comfortable doing. My husband couldn't spend the night away from home for about 5 months. I stayed in a B&B alone.
8. There is no "at least." Some people will tell you that "at least you still have each other." It's okay to still grieve and feel awful even though you still have your partner.

Making Contact

At some point we have all probably tried to make contact with our deceased children. We've probably all gone about this in different ways but the ultimate goal has been to communicate with them on some level to prove that they are "okay." I know people who have sought mediums, astrologers, psychics, and even all of those at once. The results have been mixed.

Making sense of their deaths and trying to connect with them is normal. For some people, attempting contact might even be a part of their faith. I realize that there are some people who are going to roll their eyes at this bit, but if it helps then do it.

115

Finding professionals

There are lots of people out there who claim to have the talent to reconnect us with our departed loved ones. Some of these people charge a lot of money. Sometimes, to the person seeking solace, the money is worth it. I know women who have flown all over the country to visit mediums in order to make contact with their children.

The difference between a psychic and a medium is that a medium has the ability to connect with the dead and communicate with them while a psychic does not always possess this ability. Instead, a psychic might be able to see into your future, or even into your past life. For this reason, mediums are more sought after in the cases of connecting with your child than psychics in most cases, although a good psychic might be able to do both.

An astrologer is generally not a psychic or a medium but, instead, relies on the stars to tell you about your life, future, and past. An astrologer might be able to give you information about your child's death and any future children that you might have.

Professionals can be found all over the place: the internet, classifieds, psychic or New Age fairs, recommendations from friends, etc. If you go, I would recommend looking into them first and trying to find some sort of review on them. It's best if you know someone who has visited them first and can give you a head's up on what to expect.

In some cases with mediums, you might have a private reading. In other cases you might have a group reading where the medium walks around the room and waits for spirits to come to them and talk. If you're in one of these situations then be prepared for the fact that your child might not connect with the medium so you might walk away without any contact.

The afterlife

How people feel about the afterlife varies. Some hold true to their religion's particular beliefs. You might believe in a heaven of sorts, reincarnation, a mixture of the two, or nothing at all. You might simply believe that when we die we go back to the earth and there isn't a life beyond the one that we are living.

Some people find that when they lose a child their idea of the afterlife changes. You might have once believed that when people pass on they go to Heaven and meet up with other friends and relatives and serve God. Now, however, you might be questioning that and, instead, feel like maybe your child's spirit is still hanging around you or might be reincarnated as your next child or grandchild.

Some people believe that when their babies die they remain babies for eternity and that other people in the afterlife take care of them until they can get there and do it themselves. Others believe that the soul has no age and that, in the afterlife, their child takes on the form of an adult figure.

It is not unusual to spend a lot of time thinking about the afterlife and imagining your child in it. A lot of people gain comfort thinking about their child being with angels and God, playing in Heaven's playground and flying around on perfect wings. To others, that image is not comforting at all and they would rather think of their child as coming back to life in another form and getting another chance at living again.

Don't be surprised if your beliefs change and conform as your grief changes. Like grief itself, your idea of the afterlife is not always linear.

Movies about the afterlife

Sometimes watching movies about hauntings and the afterlife has been helpful to some parents. That sense of life continuing on and the hope of one day being reconnected with your child is strong and hopeful and, for some, extremely necessary. This is a short list of movies that deal with the afterlife that you might want to consider watching, if you're looking for such a thing. Some of them do deal with child loss but others do not.

What Dreams May Come (1998)

The Sixth Sense (1999)

Made in Heaven (1987)

The Others (2001)

Child of Glass (1978)

Ghost (1990)

The Lovely Bones (2009)

Always (1989)

City of Angels (1998)

Field of Dreams (1989)

The Five People You Meet in Heaven (2004)

The Ghost and Mrs. Muir (1947)

Heart and Souls (1993)

My ideas

My ideas on the afterlife have changed a lot. I believe both in a
Summerland and reincarnation. I do not think that Toby is a
baby somewhere. I like to think that his soul is ageless and
timeless and that age itself is an earthly thing, not a spiritual
thing. I believe that the afterlife as a place is made up of what we
imagine it to be. (Kind of like the movie *What Dreams May Come*.)
I think our afterlives can overlap with other people's and that
we're able to enjoy romantic and adult relationships in it. I do
believe that we tend to travel through our lives with soul mates
and that when we are ready we are reborn back down here to
Earth and start over. I don't think we have just on soul mate, I
think we travel with a group of people.

I believe that Toby was in his Summerland for awhile.
He may or may not have been reborn yet. An astrologer I went

to said that I would see him again in this life. So maybe he will return to me as my grandchild.

I also believe in ghosts and spirits. I think that sometimes spirits can get trapped here if they have unfinished business or if their deaths were really traumatic. I don't believe all ghosts are "ghosts" however. Sometimes I think what we see and hear is merely leftover energy, like we're watching scenes from the past.

Hauntings

A lot of my friends have had paranormal experiences with their infants. I did not feel Toby's spirit for a very long time. I didn't feel like his spirit hung around and I still don't. I do, however, believe that he pops in from time to time or at least sends someone on his behalf.

Toby's anniversary was on the 21st. Last year, the day came and went. I was surprised at the lack of depression I felt. Other days had felt worse. This year, though, a couple of truly extraordinary things happened.

At around 3:00 am I was laying in bed, watching television. I had it on "mute." The "George Lopez" show was on.

I reached for the remote to turn it up, and just as I did the eldest daughter said, "I miss Tobey."

I thought that was a little strange, so I flipped over to "Sex and the City." Samantha was talking to her new boyfriend about his name and suggesting that he change it to make it something more memorable. "How about Toby?" she suggested.

Two references to Toby, back to back.

How odd, I thought.

Shrugging, I slipped on my robe and went downstairs.

When I walked into the kitchen, I was hit with a surprise. There, next to the refrigerator, was a plant leftover from Toby's funeral. In the past three hours, it had bloomed. There were five blossoms, one for each of us in our house that night.

The plant had not bloomed since Toby's funeral.

I was thankful that he had been able to send us a message that night.

There were no candles lit for us on his anniversary. The only people who sent me messages were fellow mothers who had also lost children and remembered Toby's day. We didn't do anything special to commemorate the day. But, somehow, he managed to drop in and pay us a little visit. That was enough.

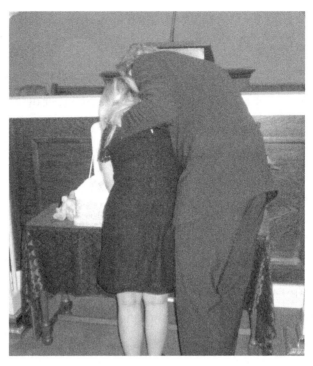

It was three years before I noticed that orb in the picture above my shoulder

My friend Wanda lost her daughter Lindsey to SIDS. Lindsey's animal totem was a ladybug. When Wanda is feeling down or sad or depressed a ladybug often lands on her and cheers her up. We like to think that it's Lindsey, checking in on her mom to see how she's doing.

Karla's experience

Many times I wished I believed I would see Kyle again, that he was indeed in a better place and was happily laughing and playing with the other children up in heaven but I just can't. I can see how comforting a belief such as this would be to one after the loss of their child but also angering that the god you love and worship needed to have YOUR child. I had to recognize that it is I, not Kyle, who needs to be in a better place, emotionally, that Kyle is gone and for his memory to live on and his life have meaning, I had to do it. I was and always will be his mother and because I don't believe I will ever see him again, I have to make the time he had here count for something.

My visit with the psychic and medium

I went to Court Day (think gigantic flea market for all you non-Kentucky people) and I had a reading done by a woman wearing a claddagh ring, pentagram necklace, and what I can only assume was a Chanel No. 5 body lacquer. Here is what followed...

We started off by having me shuffle cards, a talent I do not possess. I am like a toddler trying to crochet when it comes to shuffling. Then, she told me to pick twenty cards and that I would *know* which ones to pick. So, I fanned them out, closed my eyes, and waited for my fingers to guide me.

I got nothing.

So, I tried envisioning the things that I had questions about, visualize my questions, and try again.

Nope. Still nothing.

In the end, I just picked out twenty random cards and hoped for the best.

The first thing she asked me was if my husband and I were fighting about money. Um, nope? She was like a dog with a bone over this issue, though. "I can see there have been some disagreements. Does he make you account for every dollar you spend?" I almost snorted out my coke over that one. Pete later said that it sounded like a pretty good idea.

I just went ahead and told her that Pete's mom had passed away to see if that led to anything. "Yes, I can see her," she said. "And don't worry, she's taking care of your little boy." I must have looked confused.

"Really?" I asked. "*Really?*"

"Oh yes, I can see him with an elderly woman." Okay, Pete's Mom was like, fifty, when she died and didn't look a day over forty.

So, then I asked her what I really wanted to know: Are we attached to some negative spirit or energy? Well, she couldn't answer that, but she did tell me to burn a lot of sage and take a shower whenever we came in. In fact, she said that *all* of us needed to take a shower whenever we came inside. I am not sure if she meant together or not.

The last thing I asked her was why I was unable to get any sense of Toby, when I can tune in to just about anyone else. She said she didn't know, that maybe it was because I was too close to the situation. But she didn't offer any special messages from him.

Before I left, she assured me that you never get over the loss of a child. No kidding. She then said that she still thinks about hers. Oh, well, that was unexpected. "What happened to your child?" I asked.

"He just couldn't stay attached to the placenta," she said.

Afterwards, I found my dad and his gun booth. "Daddy, I got a reading from a psychic and it was *bad*..." I whined. So he gave me my money back. I left wondering if I had really just paid someone to call Pete's mom "elderly" and tell me to take more showers.

A year later I paid a visit to a medium. This time she was more direct. She informed me that there was a young boy surrounding me and that he was accompanied by a woman in her sixties. The boy said that I kept a memorial for him and that he was thankful for it. The woman said that she was proud of me.

I wanted to believe that this was true. But the medium could have very easily learned about my son's death from my website or blog.

Pretending to be Normal

Eventually, you have to start doing "normal" things again. For some people that happens sooner than others. Some people take a year off. Some never go back to work. With another child in the house, we at least had to go through the motions of doing normal things like bathing, cooking dinner, and picking up the place. Not that we had ever been real sticklers about some of that to begin with, though.

There are lots of reasons why you might have to "pretend" to be normal. Unfortunately, especially when it comes to working, most of us have to do it for financial reasons.

Watching our son on the playground, a month after Toby died

The financial costs of a child's death

With all of the horrible things that happen after a child's death, the last thing you want to think about is money. Yet, there it is...

You would think that with everything else going on you'd at least get a reprieve from that part of the burden, but you don't.

The funeral parlor and director cut us a break (thank goodness) and only charged us for the coffin and burial plot. In total, it was about $2500. My father-in-law paid $1,000 of that. We later paid $600 for the headstone. In expenses, we paid close to $3,000. Still, that wasn't terrible considering that funerals generally start at around $6,000.

We could not afford to take much time off from work in our grief. Toby died on Saturday, Pete started teaching on Monday. He went to all of his classes. The funeral was Wednesday and he took that day off but then went back on Thursday. I took two weeks off. My bills were all late that month.

A month after Toby died, Pete's full time job let him go. I know this made some people angry because they felt like his office should have given him some slack considering what was going on but we understood. He just couldn't do it at the time. They were nice about it, but it hit us hard.

As a result, we had to pull Sam out of daycare because we could no longer afford it. That meant that I had to crunch my forty hour workweek down to about fifteen hours. I was doing the same amount of work, but in less than half the time.

A friend had a yard sale for us and raised about $250. (The exact amount escapes me at the moment.) We used it to buy flowers for Toby's grave for Halloween, Thanksgiving, and Christmas. We also used to it pay a bill because I got behind with one of my clients when I just couldn't get out of bed for a week.

Even though the funeral costs were less than $3,000 it took us a year to pay them off. I felt so guilty visiting the cemetery and not seeing a headstone. We got one on in May (about nine months after he died) and I felt such relief.

Friends did send $25 or $50 here and there and that helped A LOT. We were very grateful for that. I lost a lot of regular clients and jobs during those first few months. I was working as hard as ever, but it took me longer and I made mistakes that needed to be corrected. With some of the money, we created a scholarship for the writer's retreat we had attended with Toby.

People said that they were sending it to help with funeral expenses and such, but what some didn't understand is that the financial burdens that come with losing a child are not limited to expenses directly associated with the death. Pete lost his job because of Toby's death. We needed money for groceries. We needed money for gas to get him back and forth to the one job he *did* have. Some of our friends understood that. One even sent me a check for $30 and told me *not* to use it for anything except taking myself to get a manicure or something. Pete and I went to the movies.

For weeks, we ate nothing but plain chicken legs, canned beans, and pasta. I made a lot of tea.

We are still feeling the financial effects of his death. We don't even live paycheck to paycheck anymore. Some months, we have no idea where our money is coming from. I have pawned my wedding ring, sold the designer dresses I collected when I was younger, and held so many yard sales that we barely have any furniture left. We sold our living room furniture, our desk, bedroom furniture, and our dining room set. Pete sold his brand new riding mower. We mowed our seven acres with a push mower. He sold off his knife collection in order to pay our car insurance.

He has been unable to find a new full time job like the one he lost when Toby died, though.

On top of everything else, it sucks that we think of money and financial hardship in regards to our son's death. Losing a child sends you on a downwards spiral in so many ways. We are just now starting to get back on our feet.

When I see a family that has lost a child I now look at them differently. Not only is there the emotional damage, but there's the humiliation of the financial struggle on top of that to contend with.

My experience

For the first week people were in and out all the time. They scrubbed our toilets, cooked meals, took me to doctors' appointments, watched movies with us...Then that stopped. People had lives and everything. After that we kind of floundered. What were we supposed to do next?

Many people took it upon themselves to try to "fix" me. I'd had plenty of time to grieve, two weeks is enough apparently, and so now it was time to make me "better." People wrote me and asked me if they could bring me books on what it was like to have a stillborn, pamphlets on panic disorders and anxiety, and Hospice information. (I thought that last one was weird until I found out they had a program for bereaved parents.) Others came over and wanted to play counselor with me. Some of my former co-workers seemed stiff around me and used words and phrases that we had learned in training sessions together, like I was a client. It made me nervous.

People seemed to either want to psychoanalyze me or completely ignore the fact that Toby died. There were very few folks who walked that happy medium. They either seemed to be amazed at the fact that we were getting out and doing so much (this was before I became agoraphobic) or admonishing us for not "moving on." It was all very confusing.

I did my best to put on a show when I could. Although I could definitely break out in tears at any given moment, and did quite frequently, I also laughed and joked and tried to do fun things. We took our son to the circus, we did our annual fall festivals, I went out drinking with friends on Halloween and even dressed up, I had a Halloween party for my friends with kids...We did what we could.

Carving pumpkins with the family 2 months after Toby's death

I faked being normal. It helped. There were days when I literally couldn't get out of bed. My sadness manifested itself in physical ailments: headaches, joint pain, vomiting, and other aches and pains. On top of the fact that I had a very real brain disorder which also caused these things to begin with, there were days when I couldn't function. I gave into those days a lot. It did not make me feel good, though, because as bad as I felt nothing felt worse than the guilt I felt in regards to my parenting skills. I needed to be a better mother and I just couldn't be; that made me feel awful.

I did not want to die, but I certainly didn't want to live the way I was living any longer, either. Doctors only wanted me to go to counseling. I needed drugs-the legal kind. In hindsight I can see that I really needed medical intervention. My panic attacks got so awful that I got to where I could barely leave the house. I was never prescribed anything for them. I believe that extra help would have set me on a better path really early on. I didn't understand why other parents who lost kids were getting valium, klonopin, and antidepressants when I had nothing. I felt like an addict for even asking.

Things did get bad for awhile. I started cutting myself. I wasn't trying to kill myself, but the physical signs that I'd had Toby were gone. I lost the pregnancy weight, my boobs shrunk, and my period came back. I needed a physical manifestation of my pain. Cuts helped that. They scared me but for a moment they gave me something else to concentrate on.

The thought of dying and leaving my son behind terrified me. Yet I didn't know what to do about it. Every day it felt like I was walking through molasses, barely moving. My thoughts were in a fog. People told me to focus on the happy memories but I swear that was worse than thinking about the bad times. I could envision Toby being blue and the blood running out of his little nose and all that horrible stuff and not shed a tear. But then I would think about his smile and I felt like I could cry for days.

My husband said that having to deal with people on a regular basis, and basically getting out of the house not only forced him to get back into a "normal" routine but also made him have to wear a "second face." Because obviously he couldn't go to class and teach looking all depressed and stuff. I didn't have this problem as much since I didn't get out much. I did understand about the need to don a "second face" though. When I didn't wear it I just seemed to piss people off and sometimes run them off altogether.

My husband didn't want medication or counseling: He just wanted a couple of months to go by without something terrible happening or somebody dying. He got tired of people trying to get us to be optimistic, happy, and "fixed."

Putting flowers on his brother's grave

Casey's experience

We did not have anyone who could help us with the funeral expenses.
We paid for everything ourselves, including his final medical bills since
we didn't have insurance. That was three years ago and we're still
paying on some things.

One of the first things it took me awhile to move on from was
the jealousy that I experienced when I saw other parents with babies the
same age that Jace was-or would have been. I didn't understand why
THEY were able to keep their baby but I wasn't. Was I being punished?
What had I done wrong? It wasn't fair. I grew angry when I saw

friends of mine acting cavalier about their children and taking them for
granted. Someone wrote on FB one day that "I have three children now,
I'm doomed!" I wrote back and said, "Lucky you, I WISH I had all
three of mine here." I couldn't help myself.

I also didn't understand people who compared their child's
illness and disabilities to my child's death. Or, their child would be
away at college or stationed overseas and they would tell me that it was
"like" they were dead. No, it's not. If you can still communicate with
your child in any way and can still see them then it's NOT like they're
dead.

All a dream

Losing your infant can feel like a dream. Sometimes, for me,
even Toby himself feels like a dream.

Right away we moved all his things into his room. We
kept the door closed but there were still reminders of him all
over the house. In fact, the entire house was a reminder of him.
But in other ways, it's hard to imagine that he was ever here.
After his death I was no longer pregnant and went back to my
pre-pregnancy weight. I had no stretch marks, no swollen
breasts, and no physical signs that I was ever pregnant to start

with. My period was back after ten months of being gone. His formula has been put away, his bottles washed, and the garbage gone that contained his diapers. The house looked very much the same as it did before he was born, when we were still expecting it. It almost felt as though we were still expecting him.

People kept telling me how much I had it together, but I really didn't feel like I did. They just saw the good parts. At home, I was pretty looney. I forgot everything. I could remember to take care of Sam but I had little patience with him and that makes me sad. I could work my job fine, but I had trouble finding the motivation to take a shower (even though baths I did every night). I felt like I was moving through a fog.

Nothing felt real.

Things my friends and I have done to pretend that we feel normal

1. Gone shopping for new clothes that we promptly forget we bought.
2. Gone drinking with friends (and spent the whole night wishing we were home).
3. Gone on a trip, even though it's hard to crawl out of bed.
4. Applied makeup. Sometimes poorly.

5. Gone out on a date with our spouses.

6. Gone back to work.

7. Hosted a party to show our friends that we can still be "fun."

8. Taken our kids to birthday parties, swimming, roller skating, and the circus to prove to ourselves that we really are good parents, despite the way we might feel.

9. Cleaned house, and not because we are stress cleaners.

10. Posted cheerful status updates and pictures and refrained from talking about our dead children in an attempt to prove to everyone that we're not depressing to be around.

11. Refrained from talking about our dead children in general because we don't want to run anyone else off.

12. Changed our hair color or style so that we physically look different so as to match the fact that we feel different inside.

Going out with a friend a couple of months after Toby's death

All the Baby Stuff

You do come to a point where you have to do something with the "stuff." No matter how far you push it away from your mind, whether it's days later or years, decisions must be made. All of the baby clothes, the furniture, the toys, the leftover powder formula...What do you do with it?

Sometimes you have to go a step further and decide what to do with your entire house. Some parents are unable to keep living there, like my friend Valerie. Others couldn't fathom leaving, like me. Some parents feel so connected and tied to their babies in the house that they were living in that leaving feels like losing them again. Others are consumed by the memories and can't take it.

Many of us went on to have subsequent children. That kind of forced us to have to do something with our deceased child's belongings. For those who had extra bedrooms or didn't have subsequent children right away, it didn't matter so much. I know a few parents who lost children years ago and still haven't done anything with their rooms. Not that my opinion matters, but I think it's fine.

My experience

I was planning on bringing my subsequent child back to the house where her brother died. We loved it there. After almost eight months of awfulness we were finally starting to feel normal again. I can remember sitting on the couch one spring evening watching "Dancing with the Stars." A couple was dancing was to Miley Cyrus' "Party in the USA." My son was playing in the floor. My husband was reading a book. I was actually feeling pretty good that night and had ventured downstairs. We had the door open because it was a nice evening. It was one of the few good evenings we'd had in awhile. For the first time in a long time I thought we were going to be okay.

Our house

The next day we got a call from our landlord. His company was relocating him. He was going to need his house back. Our world fell apart again.

I was nearing my due date. Now we had to pack everything up, find a place to live, and move. I was forced not only pack Toby's things up but leave the house where his memories were on terms that weren't my own. It was awful. I cried and cried. I cried for months really. Even after we got moved my son would sometimes cry and ask when we could go "home." I didn't know what to tell him because I wanted to go "home" too.

Toby's Christmas tree (and some pictures a friend's children drew for us)

Keep in mind...

1. You don't have to listen to anyone else. It's *always* your decision as far as your baby's things are concerned.

2. You can pack it all away in boxes and go through it later. That later might be a month away or a year away. Do it when you're ready.

3. You can keep everything and anything you want, even if it doesn't make any sense. (Although disposable things like bottles with formula and used diapers really should be thrown out just as soon as you are able to do so.)

4. You can ask a friend or family member to help you, do it all on your own, or do a mixture of the two.

5. Those plastic bags with zippers that sheets and pillow cases sometimes come in make good storage for little clothes and blankets.

6. Memory boxes and shadow boxes with clothing, pacifiers, and shoes can be displayed anywhere in your house.

7. Some of the nursery decorations might look good in the rest of your house and will be a reminder of your child.

8. Don't feel obligated to reuse your child's nursery furniture for your subsequent child if you have one. We didn't. Others feel better doing so.

9. Some people like cutting up the clothing to make blankets and other things out of them. Others don't like to alter them at all.

10. A special unique chest that sets in your living room or bedroom and holds your child's clothes and blankets is a good way of keeping everything close yet out of the way.

11. Pinterest can be a good resource for repurposing furniture. We plan on using Toby's headboard as a rose trellis eventually.

12. You don't have to wash your child's dirty clothes until you're ready or not at all if you don't want to.

13. You can continue to buy things for your child. Our son's theme was a nautical one. Every year we buy a new sailboat for our office.

Toby's baby shower

Melissa's experience

I have almost of his clothes here in a storage tub. There are also clothes that he wore more regularly when he was here at my house. I kept them in the drawer in my room. There are still there now. Even though I have replaced all the furniture in my room, I still keep his clothes in the drawer. I probably always will. I don't know what I will do with the

145

clothes in the storage tub, but I know that getting rid of them is not going to ever happen. I still have his toys here that he played with. His little brother has played with them also. I am keeping them. I put some in the casket with him. He had plastic chain links that used to hang on the handle of his car seat. I now put them on my Christmas tree each year. In my closet I have a pink Kroger balloon that my granddaughter had but I asked her to let him have it because he liked it so much. She was ok with it and we played with it for hours that Friday night he stayed the night with (for the first time). He played with it, shredded the ribbon with his teeth and wiped snot all over it. He passed away on Sunday. It still has a little bit of air in it...and still snot on it no one is allowed to so much as touch it.

Wanda's memorial to Lindsey with her picture and ladybugs

The New and Totally Unofficial Stages of Grief

Almost as soon as Toby died people started sending me links regarding the "stages of grief" and what I could expect. You probably know these. They are denial, anger, acceptance, etc. I learned to have disdain for these but I've never really been able to articulate why those stages and that whole concept bothers me so much.

Some of it has to do with the fact that in the beginning, whenever I expressed an emotion it would inevitably be met with a comment like, "Oh, yeah, you're still in the bargaining stage." I hated that my grief and sadness were being chopped down to analytical expressions.

Plus, I never really resonated with the stages themselves. I never went through a bargaining period. With Toby gone, what was there to bargain with? I woke up and he was already dead. There was no praying to bring him back or making empty promises to do better.

Later, I learned that the stages themselves were originally created to deal with a traumatic illness, not death at all. This made more sense to me. I can say that now having dealt with a brain problem, those stages are much more fitting to that process than they ever were to losing my child.

I have also learned that if there is a cycle it is not linear. You can jump around and go back to the different stages and you don't even have to do them in order. That makes more sense, too. The original model for the stages of grief does not take cultural relevance or an individual's specific support system or interpersonal relationships into account. I do believe this is important to consider.

The reason it's important is because if you read a lot of child loss blogs you will see that most of us have different ways of dealing with things. These differences can be significant. It's also important to remember that grief from child loss is *never-ending*. You might reach an acceptance stage and stay there for months or years and then go back to anger again. There are no "rules" as to how this works.

So I have been researching and reading and I have come across some other theories and ideas about the stages of complicated grief and I wanted to share them. I have totally made these up based on my own experiences, experiences of others, and research.

1. Adrenalin rush

I guess this could also be grouped in with shock. I do, however, believe that it was the "fight or flight" response that got me through the first few days of Toby's death. The rush of adrenalin enabled me to perform CPR, hold the breathing tube in his mouth in the ambulance, wipe the blood from his mouth and nose in the hospital, make all the phone calls, and make important decisions such as organ donations hours after his death. It was more than numbness-it was a *rush*. I felt like a go, go, go movement inside of me until I eventually collapsed back at home. This rush of sorts continued on, albeit at a slower pace, for several months.

2. Searching

Some might call this denial, but I think it's more biological than emotional. In the weeks following Toby's death, I still biologically felt like a new mother. I felt weight in my arms, heard his cries, and occasionally found myself wrapping up pillows and swaddling them without even thinking about it. My body was still on his sleep schedule. I believe that I was unconsciously searching for the baby that was no longer there. I compare this to the same way that our body tells us that we need food, hydration, or sleep.

3. Numbness

I personally lived with numbness for months. Although I was still crying on a daily basis and certainly felt sad, it all felt in my head. It hadn't touched my heart yet. The numbness allowed me to make decisions, cook dinner, play with Sam, and do all of the little things that seemed insignificant at the time. Sometimes, even a couple of years later, that numbness still pervades.

4. Suffering

The real suffering set in months later-probably at about the six month mark. That's when the real pain, agitation, depression, loneliness, and guilt came on in full force. The reality of the situation was clear and enough time had passed that everything in me knew that he was gone for good and was not coming back. These were, by far, the hardest months for me. Unfortunately, I think for most people, by the time this comes around a good deal of their support people are gone so while this might be the toughest "stage", it's usually one that is faced alone.

5. Anger

I would say that the anger was always there, but it came on really strong once the suffering hit. To be clear, I was NEVER angry at Toby. My anger was directed at other people. I was angry at the way we were treated directly after his death, angry at the way we continued to be treated, and angry at the people around me who had all pulled away.

This might not be a popular viewpoint, but sometimes directing my anger at other people made me feel better. As long as I was angry I still had feelings and wasn't numb. That's not to say that those people didn't deserve my anger, because they did, but I think my anger served a purpose as well. To be mad at them for not understanding, for brushing us off, and for seemingly not to care I could harness my emotions and have an outlet. In the long run, did it matter that those insignificant people didn't understand me? No. But I didn't have anything else to do with those feelings.

6. Loss of faith

I don't necessarily mean this in the religious sense. I think at this point people can start questioning their faith in many things:

their religion, their friends, their family, their goodwill, and the world in general. It becomes difficult to see the good in things around you. You are no longer innocent and naive. You KNOW that building a brick house is no longer a surefire way of keeping the big bad wolf from blowing it down. Your very foundation is rocked. Some people come out of this stronger in faith. Some never do.

6. Adjusting

Recovery, also called "acceptance", does not mean that we have moved on from our grief. It doesn't really even mean that we have "recovered" from it since you NEVER recover from losing a child. I think what it DOES mean is that you manage to find a somewhat healthy way of living with it in better harmony. The things that used to prevent you from doing something, like going to a park and seeing other children playing, still hurt like hell, but you manage to find a way of doing them with some level of functionality.

7. Reorganization

This is a relatively new one for me but it makes sense. There came a point where it became very important for me to organize not only Toby's things but my life in general. I wanted to sort through his clothing and toys, clean up my Facebook friends, and scrub the toilet all on the same day. Putting things in order is a huge part of the grieving process and still something that strikes me at odd times. I got a lot of comfort out of folding his clothes, wrapping them in plastic, making shadowboxes, and creating a scrapbook. On the same token, I got a similar sense of fulfillment by dusting, vacuuming, and cleaning out my shoes. It might have something to do with regaining a sense of control, but I'd rather not analyze it too much.

Acceptance

I am not including this as a stage. I am adding it, though, because sometimes one of the hardest parts of dealing with grief is being able to accept that we are in a "new" normal. I know it sounds strange, but sometimes we have to grieve the act of moving on from a grieving stage.

It can be incredibly hard to go from crying every day and feeling horrible to suddenly...not. In fact, that can make us feel WORSE. It brings on all kinds of guilt. That's why it's so important to be gentle with ourselves.

There are some mothers I know who are unable to read grief blogs from those who are newly grieving because it makes them feel as though they are slipping backwards. It's important to remember that's okay, too. Even though we have all experienced a loss, none of our losses are the same. Everyone is on their own path, has to find their own way, and may or may not feel the same way about things.

KEEP IN MIND

* Grief has no set time limits-you will always be grieving
* There are no "true" stages-everyone grieves differently and not every "stage" will apply to every person
* We will never be our "old selves" again, but that doesn't mean that there can't be wonderful things that we find in our "new normal."

Hurting Ourselves

Suicide is not a pleasant topic, but it's one that comes up a lot. Right away, after Toby died, people seemed to watch me a little more closely than usual. I didn't feel suicidal. I didn't want to die. I didn't want to live, but I didn't want to die either.

But then, one day, I thought about killing myself.

My experience

It was not a well thought out plan. It wasn't a plan at all. But I did think about it. I thought about it a lot. I had friends I could call but they were busy and working and I felt like a burden. And one friend that I did talk to on a regular basis generally made me feel worse for reasons I won't go into.

The suicidal thoughts started the week I was accused of killing my baby. I was also accused of killing Pete's mom and causing the death of his father (who incidentally is still alive so apparently I'm not that good yet). In addition, I was called "disturbed" a "piece of work" and other things that I hate to think about now. This all came from my husband's family and (now former) friends. In addition, I was accused of running Pete's friends off, of keeping him from going to England for his mother's funeral, of stifling his future, and we were sent a bill for thousands of dollars for the money that has been "invested" in Pete over the years by his family. One message I received said that I wasn't a "real mother" because a "real mother" would have let Pete leave.

I know all of this is hard to understand now, but Pete's mother died two weeks after Toby died. We made plans for the three of us to fly over for the funeral. I was getting a hotel room for us and had contacted some of our friends in England to come and visit so that Pete could spend time with his family. Drama ensued when his father informed us that he didn't want Sam and I to come and that our presence was not welcomed. Since Pete had just lost his youngest son and was depressed, he couldn't stand the thought of leaving us behind. We needed to be together. He chose not to leave us if he couldn't bring us.

Pete received a range of messages from friends and family, telling him that he should have gone home. I booked the ticket for him. I booked the car rental for him. I even kissed him good bye. He was the one that ultimately made the decision not to get in the car. And he had his reasons. Pete's friends and family members might not have agreed with his decision, but they sure as hell should have supported him. And they shouldn't have added to our grief like they did.

I was told that at least I had Pete, Mom, and Sam to return to at the end of the day but that all Pete's dad has to return to was an empty house.

I didn't feel that way. I had a room full of baby clothes that will never be worn. I had bottles that would never be used again. I had a can of formula, half full, that would never be used up the rest of the way. I had an opened bag of diapers that rested on a changing table that wouldn't see a baby. I had a nursery decorated in sailboats that would never hear laughter or the cries of a little one. I had a backpack, meant for our outings, that would never have little feet dangling from it. I had signs all over our house that a baby WAS there, but there was no baby. I had a son that saw me crying and hugged me and asked, "Do you miss your baby" and then asked my mother if Mommy was going away, too. That's what I had every day.

Somedays, it was too much to take a shower or a bath. Somedays, it was all I could do to get out of bed. I had panic attacks that resulted in Pete having to throw blankets and bathrobes over me because I couldn't get enough weight on me. I hid in the closet and shut the door because the room was too bright. I couldn't sleep at night because the last time I slept all the way through the night my son died while I slept.

Coupled with the anger and negativity from friends and family, I couldn't take it anymore. I started believing the hype that was coming at me. I started believing that I was a bad person, that I DID somehow cause the death of my son, that I was disturbed, that I was a piece of work, and that I DID stop Pete from going to the funeral of his mother.

I never planned my death, but I sure thought about it a lot. I wished for it. And then I took to cutting myself. The cuts

157

gave me something physical to do and look at. The worst I felt, the more I cut.

Finally, one day, it just stopped. There was no magic cure. (Well, there kind of was. We cut out almost everyone in our lives.) One day I just woke up and felt better. I don't know how I survived. I think it was luck.

When you're feeling like you want to die

1. If you have anxiety medication or pain pills, give them to your partner and ask them to dispense them to you.
2. Have a friend on alert. Make sure it's someone you can call at all hours of the night.
3. Don't mix alcohol with medication as this might cause an adverse reaction.
4. Bathe with the door open. Ask a friend or spouse to sit in the bathroom with you.
5. Journal. Blog. Write in something.
6. Get out of the house. Go for a walk, a movie, a drive...just remove yourself from the location you're in.
7. Talk to your doc. Sometimes the medication they prescribe for anxiety and depression can have the opposite effect on some people.

8. If you have kids, ask someone you trust to take them for a few days.

9. Pamper yourself. Watch an old movie, stay in bed, eat junk. Do nothing.

10. Sleep. Sometimes things look better in the morning. Sometimes they don't. But sleep often has a way of reprogramming us.

If these thoughts continue, please seek help. It doesn't have to be scary, I swear. I also have fears of the psych ward and mental hospitals, thank you horror movies, but it's really just about having someone to talk to you in your own doctor's office.

Jenny's experience

I thought about suicide a lot in the beginning. I never got to the planning stage, but I definitely thought about dying more than the average person does. My dream was to go to sleep and just not wake up again. I did think about ways that it could be done. Guns scared me and I was afraid I might put it in the wrong place and, instead of dying, make myself a vegetable or something. I didn't want to run my car off the road for the same reason. I figured they'd just pump my stomach if I overdosed. I didn't know about cutting my wrists or using the whole tube through the car window thing.

One of the main reasons I wanted to die was because I felt so damn guilty all the time. I felt guilty because I knew I was being a terrible parent to my other two kids and a lousy wife. I did not see things getting better. People would tell me to just "think about the kids" but that's when I wanted to die the most. Thinking about them did not make me want to live-thinking about them made me think they would be better off without me.

I talked to a few friends about feeling suicidal. One deleted me from Facebook and then told everyone I was "too much drama."

I finally went to my doctor. She gave me something for anxiety. It helped. Mostly by knocking me out when I was feeling the worst. Other than that time was really the only thing that helped.

Depression, anxiety, & other things

It's no surprise that losing your child can send you over the emotional edge but along with everything else it can also affect your mental health and give you issues that you've never dealt with before. Mental health problems still have a terrible stigma attached to them but there is no need to be ashamed of seeking help for them. The help doesn't always have to be in the form of drugs and counseling. There are natural methods of decreasing the symptoms to some of the most common mental health problems, but when things become too much to handle then calling in the pros might be on the table.

Symptoms of Depression

Depression has been an accepted part of the stages of grief for awhile now, but depression can come in different forms. Not all depression leads to suicidal thoughts and not all depressed people feel sad. Sometimes, lack of interest in activities and a feeling of helplessness are signs of depression.

Depression is different from simply feeling sad. Depression kicks in after a little bit of time has gone by and the symptoms of it are gradual. They might worsen or remain steady. There are lots of ways of treating depression. Some people choose not to use any chemicals in treating it. Others need them. If you find that one treatment option is not working for you or has stopped working then you should discuss other ways of managing your symptoms with your healthcare provider.

According to the NIMH's website at
http://www.nimh.nih.gov/health/topics/depression/men-and-depression/signs-and-symptoms-of-depression/index.shtml the
symptoms of depression include:

- Persistent sad, anxious, or "empty" mood
- Feelings of hopelessness, pessimism
- Feelings of guilt, worthlessness, helplessness
- Loss of interest or pleasure in hobbies and activities
- Decreased energy, fatigue, being "slowed down"
- Difficulty concentrating, remembering, making decisions
- Difficulty sleeping, early-morning awakening, or oversleeping
- Appetite and/or weight changes
- Thoughts of death or suicide; suicide attempts
- Restlessness, irritability
- Persistent physical symptoms

Symptoms of Anxiety

There are different types of anxiety and just about everyone suffers from some kind of it after losing their child. Many people end up having acute panic attacks, though, and these can be scary. Your anxiety might hit you at different times and be triggered by different things. It might also get better for awhile and then worsen.

The different types of anxiety include: panic disorders, performance anxiety, generalized anxiety disorder, obsessive-compulsive disorder, social anxiety, phobias, and PTSD.

Some of us experience agoraphobia and social anxiety after losing our child, even though we never had a problem being out of the house and around people in the past. I went through this for about four months and it was excruciating. At its worst, a friend came all the way from Alabama and wanted to meet us at a restaurant. I got dressed and then couldn't step outside the door. She totally understood and brought dinner to us instead.

Common symptoms of anxiety include:
- Feeling apprehensive
- Feeling powerless
- Having a sense of impending danger, panic or doom

- Having an increased heart rate
- Breathing rapidly (hyperventilation)
- Sweating
- Trembling
- Feeling weak or tired

(Information gained from The Mayo Clinic's website at http://www.mayoclinic.com/health/anxiety/DS01187/DSECTION =symptoms)

Symptoms of PTSD

Unfortunately, the diagnosis of PTSD (post traumatic stress disorder) is thrown around a lot these days. It used to apply to those who came back from war and were exposed to the atrocities of battle. These days, people get diagnosed with PTSD for things that seem a lot less significant. As a result, it's not always taken as seriously as it should be. Let me be clear here: losing your child is a serious cause for PTSD and, as a result, should be taken seriously. If you have the signs and symptoms of it and your healthcare provider does not take you seriously then you need to look elsewhere.

The following information was taken from the NIMH's (National Institute of Mental Health) website at: http://www.nimh.nih.gov/health/publications/post-traumatic-stress-disorder-ptsd/index.shtml

1. **Re-experiencing symptoms:**
   - Flashbacks—reliving the trauma over and over, including physical symptoms like a racing heart or sweating
   - Bad dreams
   - Frightening thoughts.

Re-experiencing symptoms may cause problems in a person's everyday routine. They can start from the person's own thoughts and feelings. Words, objects, or situations that are reminders of the event can also trigger re-experiencing.

2. **Avoidance symptoms:**
   - Staying away from places, events, or objects that are reminders of the experience
   - Feeling emotionally numb
   - Feeling strong guilt, depression, or worry
   - Losing interest in activities that were enjoyable in the past
   - Having trouble remembering the dangerous event.

Things that remind a person of the traumatic event can trigger avoidance symptoms. These symptoms may cause a person to change his or her personal routine. For example, after a bad car accident, a person who usually drives may avoid driving or riding in a car.

3. Hyperarousal symptoms:

- Being easily startled
- Feeling tense or "on edge"
- Having difficulty sleeping, and/or having angry outbursts.

Hyperarousal symptoms are usually constant, instead of being triggered by things that remind one of the traumatic event. They can make the person feel stressed and angry. These symptoms may make it hard to do daily tasks, such as sleeping, eating, or concentrating.

It's natural to have some of these symptoms after a dangerous event. Sometimes people have very serious symptoms that go away after a few weeks. This is called acute stress disorder, or ASD. When the symptoms last more than a few weeks and become an ongoing problem, they might be PTSD. Some people with PTSD don't show any symptoms for weeks or months.

Dealing with Other People

Dealing with other people has to be one of the hardest parts of grief. Sometimes we feel like if other people would just stop being assholes about everything we would actually do a lot better. Tragedies seem to bring out both the best and the worst in folks and I believe that those of us who have lost infants have seen it all.

One thing we tend to hear over and over again is that people "mean well." But what does that mean, exactly? That it's okay to be insensitive and say hurtful things as long as their intentions are good? As grieving parents, a lot is asked of us. Being forgiving is one of them.

The disappearing souls

For the first two weeks, my house was flooded with people trying to help. Then it just stopped. Oh, sure, there were some friends who popped by now and again but even that stopped after awhile. (To be fair, the ones who really made an effort after those first two weeks are the ones who are still around even three years later.)

I have a few theories as to why this happened. For one thing, with social media it's much easier to make contact with people superficially. People didn't have to visit or meet me or anything because they could see me online and feel as though they had done their friend duty by commenting on my status or whatnot.

Then, of course, there was my blog which managed to piss almost everyone off at some point. I did write a lot about people. Sometimes I look back on that and cringe.

As I met other grieving parents, though, I learned that it's kind of normal for people to drop off the face of the earth. They're around for a little while and then they just disappear. They can't keep up with us and our grief. It's too much for them. Our real grief doesn't really start until about six months in and by that time we've worn everyone out. They have moved on. We haven't. We don't even want to. This creates a problem.

Sometimes, people would write me or call me and say, "I'm so worried about you!" or "I wish there was something I could do!" But I never actually saw those people. And then someone would call and say, "I'm bringing over some flowers for Sam to plant outside and some dinner. Six o'clock fine?" Or someone else write and say, "What day this week you want me to come over?" Those are things I could deal with. When my seventy-five year old aunt calls me and tells me she's worried and that she loves me, I know it's real. When someone down the road does it yet I haven't seen them in months and it kind of ends there, I wonder.

I actually had an experience that still kind of hurts me, too. I was agoraphobic for awhile after Toby's death and I didn't get out much. There was an author I really liked, though, and we had exchanged a few emails over the course of the year. When I told her about Toby she even gave me her phone number. Although it was hard for me to get out of the house, when I heard she was doing a reading I made a point of going, even though it was an hour away.

This author followed my blog and seemed like a great person. Not long after that reading, though, she stopped following me and when I wrote her a friendly email she wrote back, terse and cryptic. Later, when she made a Facebook fan page, I commented on something she posted (a nice comment) and she deleted it.

All of this hurt me in ways that I can't even understand or explain. But it felt like I was being dumped again because of my child's death.

Playing therapist

Another strange phenomenon that I encountered is what I think of as the "counselor phenomenon." Suddenly it seemed like everyone wanted to come to me with their problems. I mean, *seriously*? People were actually coming to me with *their* problems and expected me to either be completely understanding or to, God bless them, *help* them. Now, I could almost understand this a few months after his death but that's not the way it happened. No, I had people doing this before the funeral even occurred. Bizarre.

Other parents have expressed the same confusion. I have a couple of theories on this. Maybe some people felt like we would be more understanding than most since we are going through something ourselves (never mind that it isn't even remotely similar).

In some cases it might have been guilt. The night before the funeral someone wrote me an almost belligerent and forceful e-mail, telling me not to be angry that they couldn't attend and then gave me a laundry list of reasons why. Another friend wrote me nearly every day after Toby's death, badgering me about her problems at work, with her boss, with her family, etc. She eventually deleted me. I guess I wasn't helpful enough.

Disappointment

Dealing with the disappointment of people is tough. Sometimes you feel like cutting off everyone except for the people you live with and starting over. People are always going to have their opinions and think that you're not doing things the way that you should. I just tried to learn to deal with that and continue to do things the way that felt right for me.

And in truth, although it might have sounded as though I was very angry and bitter, and a lot of times I was, really I was just disappointed. I was really disappointed in people that I counted on and believed in. But was that my fault or theirs? Were my expectations too high? Were they unrealistic? These were things I wondered.

Melissa's experience

Pretty much everyone was very careful with their words following this tragedy. Some just said "There are no words". That was probably the best thing they could have said. Some outright stupid things came out of people's mouths later down the road though. I went to see a shrink recently for sleep medication and I told her the story about Scooter (still need help with sleep). I also told her that I am caring for my granddaughter. Her comment to me was, "Oh, I see. You have your Granddaughter because of your Grandson's death?" I said he died of SIDS! He was not murdered! This is a "health care professional" right?

April's experience

I was so disappointed in the people in my life after my child died. I swear it was like a big black hole came and swallowed them all up. I don't know where the hell everyone went but they sure weren't around me. I tried to be understanding at first but then I got really upset. I probably shouldn't have, but I wrote some Facebook posts about it, too. I was lonely and feeling isolated and sad but people got mad at those posts and, instead of reaching out to me, deleted me. Most of them I never heard from again.

I felt really bad because I got into an argument with one friend and told her exactly how I felt about her absence. Looking back, I know I said some things I shouldn't have. I wrote her and apologized and thanked her for all of the things that she DID do but she didn't write me back.

Traumatizing situations

Sometimes the situations can just be downright traumatizing when you're dealing with other people.

I don't mind other kids asking me questions about Toby or mentioning him. This has never bothered me. In most situations, if the child asks a question about Toby in front of me then I try to answer it as best as I can and move on. It usually works. There have been a few instances, however, where it was turned into a total nightmare. In one situation, the child in question actually stood over Iris shouting, "Toby's dead, he died, he's dead, Toby's dead...and YOU might die, too!" If that had been my child, I would have been mortified. I would have apologized to the parent, been embarrassed, and at the very least changed the subject. This parent, however, sat there and laughed and kept saying, "I know, honey, he's gone, but we still love him." Had I not snapped at the poor kid, he would have kept going.

This totally traumatized me.

In other situations, the parent has started telling their child, in front of me, that Toby is dead and that he's in Heaven and we'll see him again someday. They have this whole conversation, kind of unprovoked, right there in my face while I'm kind of helplessly sitting there, ignored.

I would say that if you're going to have a theological discussion about my child's death with your own child then at least try not to do it in my presence.

That is *not* adorable.

I hate to be all "don't do this and don't do that" to a grieving parent, because nobody likes to be around a person you have to walk on eggshells around, but there HAS to be a certain level of sensitivity here.

I think it's very important to remember that many parents, including myself, suffer from PTSD or at least some form of anxiety. Allowing your child to stand over them, telling them that their child is dead, is almost certainly going to be a trigger for something. Not all grieving parents want to have theological discussions with children who aren't their own when it comes to their child's death, either. This is something we have to be respectful of.

Yes, I DO have these discussions with my own son. And occasionally he has questions. But he's my child. My suggestion would be that until you know how the parent feels about such discussions, it's something you might want to have with your children in private.

I can definitely handle this better now, but in the beginning I didn't want to listen to other children dancing around, singing about how Toby is dead. I know that they're kids and that they probably don't even understand what they're saying, but in a fragile emotional state, it's not cool.

Lori's experience

Not long after Lila died a friend sent me a picture that her daughter had drawn for me. Her daughter is five and the picture was of me and my husband with an angel (I guess it was meant to be Lila?) floating above us. It freaked me out. I know it was supposed to be cute and sensitive and that I should have appreciated her for even thinking of us at all but at the time I didn't feel that way. Instead, I threw the drawing away. I couldn't look at it. Whenever we were around this child she would always ask a million questions about Lila's death and her mom would just sit there. I wanted to be open with her, and goodness knows she showed more interest than most people, but I it made me have panic attacks. I just wasn't ready for that.

Fielding questions

"How many children do you have?" We have all been asked that question before. Some of us get it on a regular basis. If I'm out with only one of mine, I get asked if they're my only child. If I'm out with both I get asked how Sam likes being a big brother to Iris.

So how do you answer?

I say answer in whatever way you feel comfortable.

I personally don't use the term "angel baby." I know that some people answer that they have a baby in Heaven and two living. Or however it may be.

Others will exclude the child that they lost altogether. (Pete does this sometimes.)

Me? I volunteer it. "I have two living children and one that passed away when he was two months old."

I used to say that I had one living child but people assumed that my non-living child was a miscarriage. This made me uncomfortable. Although I admit that having a miscarriage is sad, I've had one myself, I can't compare the loss of that pregnancy to the loss of the child whose personality I got to know. I'm not saying that one loss is worse than another, mind you, just different. Apples and oranges.

Some people have gone so far as to argue with me about Toby and his time on this earth. This was taken from an actual conversation with a nurse during Iris' pregnancy:

Nurse: How many living children?

Me: One.

Nurse: So your abortion...

Me: What?! He wasn't an abortion!

Nurse: Oh, that's just the technical term.

Me: But-

Nurse: So how far along were you when you had your spontaneous abortion?

Me: He WASN'T an abortion!

Nurse: It's a MEDICAL term. It's doesn't mean what you think. I just need to know how far in your pregnancy you were.

Me: I KNOW what it means. It means a miscarriage. And what I am trying to tell YOU is that he was NOT a miscarriage.

Nurse: I'm sorry. So he was a stillbirth. How much premature was he?

Me: He was NOT a stillbirth! He was born. He lived. He lived for two months. And then he died. He was not a pregnancy loss.

So you get the idea.

Anyway, I differentiate when I answer the question. I say that I have two living children and one that passed away.

Sam is much more direct in this. He'll voluntarily say, "Toby died."

It does, on occasion, make people feel uncomfortable. It sometimes makes me feel sad. It also makes me feel good, though. I LIKE mentioning Toby. By not including him I feel like I am ignoring him. By counting him (but not mentioning that he is deceased) I feel like I am not honoring his passing.

Still, you should do what you feel comfortable with. Use the terminology you like and say as much or as little as you want.

There are lots of questions that get thrown our way that are hard to answer. Some of the most common ones are:

How did he/she die?

Was he/she sick?

How many kids do you have?

Are you going to have another baby?

Are you doing okay now?

Did they know or forget?

Not long ago I ran into someone I hadn't seen since before Toby's death. To put it more accurately, I hadn't seen this person since before Toby's *birth*. We spent a few minutes talking, pleasantly surprised to see one another, and they commented on Sam and Iris who were with me. No mention was made of Toby at all, which I'm kind of used to at this point, but I was curious this time. Did they forget that I'd had another child and that child had died? Or had they even known to begin with? While it was highly possible that they had not known of his birth and subsequent death, it was highly unlikely. We hadn't seen each other in a few years but we had mutual friends who had attended his funeral.

So, I asked. "Did you know I'd had another child between the two?"

They hesitated. "Yes, I did know that you had one that had passed away," they answered at last.

Huh.

Well, *that* was interesting.

In the past it might have hurt my feelings that this person had known and not only had they not contacted me but they didn't bring it up when they saw me. This time, however, it didn't bother me. I thought it was kind of funny, really, like the big white elephant in the room. I knew that my child had died and they knew that I'd had a child that died but nothing had been done by either one of us in regards to this fact toward one another in the past few years.

So, I just shrugged. Oh well. I changed the subject and we carried on.

Sometimes it is easy to wonder if people forgot that your child died. By the way they avoid mentioning them or act as though everything is going great you wonder if they forgot or even knew to begin with. One friend told me that when people do this to her she wants to jump up and down and start shouting her son's name, just to get a reaction.

Stupid things people say

And then, of course, there are the stupid things that people say.

Early on I had a "friend" write me and say, "Hope you are doing well!" That really set me off. No, thank you, I am *not* doing well. In the past four months I have lost my son, Pete lost his mother, Dad had a heart attack, Mom had a stroke, our dogs got poisoned, friends and family members who should have been supportive have acted like morons, Pete lost his job at the law office, and I got gallstones. But really, thanks for contacting me. So I basically wrote back and said that. They then replied and said that they understood, that their boyfriend had been in a car accident but he was "okay." Really? Really! That's how you "understand?" The friend also wrote Mom and said that she would like to see us more, but that she'd had a lot of things going on in the past few months. Oh, yes. Please, *please* tell us all about the things that you've had going on. Because we really want to hear it.

I got angry, too, at some things that people say regarding his death. "He's in a better place." Better than what? Better than here with us? Better than being in a place where people love him and take care of him? Okay, so obviously I am not religious in a Christian sense so those words do not offer comfort to me. Or, "It was his time to go." Really? At seven weeks he had lived out his life completely? I had a hard time believing that.

And then there was the: "Since he was a baby you can probably get a cheap headstone and just save your money. You don't have to get an expensive one."

Crazy Things People Said to Me and Others

1. At least he was a baby so you didn't get too attached to him.
2. Just think of the money you'll save on diapers.
3. You can always have another one.
4. I guess it was meant to be.

5. Did you forget to put him on his back?

6. Did you get the chance to name him before he died?
    (This to a woman who lost her 6 month old son.)

7. Some good will come of this.

8. Just read (insert Bible verse) and you'll feel a lot better.

9. At least...

10. I know how you feel. My dog/grandma/bird/great
    aunt/bus driver died and I...

11. Be strong.

12. It was their time to go.

13. Are you still upset?

14. At least you still have your other child...

Anger at others

Then there's anger. It's often directed at different people.
Sometimes it is directed at random people for no particular
reason. I tried to stay angry at the doctors because I figured
they're pretty safe to be angry at. If they had taken me seriously
maybe I wouldn't have delivered prematurely. But then again, if
I hadn't delivered prematurely then maybe we would have only
had two weeks with Toby and not seven.

I also got angry at family and friends. Like, why wasn't my sister at the visitation or funeral? Why haven't I even heard from her? Sure, we didn't grow up together and we're only half-sisters, but still...? And where was my best friend of twenty years who just lived down the road? I would get angry for no particular reason. But the anger was as hard to control as the crying and sadness.

I got on the phone with someone and she immediately went into a rampage about how all of this had happened for a reason, that Pete and I needed to help each other out, and that Sam probably needed counseling. All I'd said was "hello." That made me mad.

Kira's experience

This year I find myself so angry at everyone. The insensitive nature of people has made me wish they will experience just an hour of my pain. I will never be the exciting, fun person that I was. Even when I smile there seems to always be a shadow nearby, a shadow of pain that clouds everything around. Today, the intensity of this pain brought me back to the very early days when all I wanted was to sleep and wish I was gone as well. This is no life to live like this. And I'm asking God please we need this to be over. I want the end to come. I need to see my baby

183

again. How is it that people live with this pain with this emptiness for so many years?

Religious stuff

For some people, the religious stuff that people say is helpful. It comforts them to talk of angels and heaven and the Bible. For those of us who are not religious or do not hold those beliefs, though, it's not comforting. Living in a fairly religious area, I listened to more than one person talk to me about how it was "God's plan" and how Toby was "an angel" now and I should be "thankful" for his death. How I dealt with this depended upon the speaker and how I was feeling at the time.

I actually grew resentful of this after a time. I got tired of listening to other people's beliefs about my son, especially when they weren't at all interested in hearing about my beliefs. What I grew to understand was that what they were saying was more about them than it was about me. It didn't make it less annoying, though.

Religion is really a topic that you should try to stay away from when talking to someone who has lost a child because it is potentially explosive. I believe that unless you absolutely know that the person will be comforted by their faith or talk of religion then you just shouldn't go there. It's a complicated topic, even for those who have a lot of faith. And while it might comfort the person doing the talking, the situation really shouldn't be about them.

Karla's experience

I've been lucky not to hear too many religious comments but I've tried to take the ones I have received with a grain of salt. I understand that most people don't know what to say to someone that has lost a loved one, especially a child, and when religion has been ingrained in them all their life that's all they can think of to go to. I got a lot of the "I'm praying for you" comments and a simple thank you was all I ever responded. I appreciated the sentiment and took it as they were just thinking about us or that we were still on their mind. For the most part I've just tried to ignore the religious aspect and take it as them just trying to offer words of comfort, since no words made it any better anyway.

The eternal optimists

I had an epiphany during the writing of this book and I couldn't wait to sit down and write it out. During my subsequent pregnancy I had a lot of problems. More about that later. People were just so damn optimistic though. No matter what went wrong there was always someone there telling me to be "more positive" and that "everything would be fine." This did not make me feel good. In fact, it made me feel like I was being dismissed and ignored. Like my fears weren't valid.

As a parent who has lost a child, we've seen the worst happen. And while we want to be optimistic that it won't happen again, we are no longer naïve or innocent in this. We know that bad things can happen and that they do. The wool is no longer pulled over our eyes.

The eternal optimists did not feel like real friends to me. They felt like people who didn't want to hear my problems so they brushed me off with a wave and went on their merry way. Of course, these were also the folks who constantly complained about every little thing in their own lives. So maybe it was the hypocrisy that bothered me as well.

Anyway...a few weeks ago a SIDS mother that I am friends with found out she was pregnant. She started writing to me about her concerns regarding the pregnancy. As her friend, my instinct was to make her feel better and tell her that everything was going to be okay. I realized quickly, however, that she didn't want to hear those things. No, she wanted someone to agree with her. So I did. I commiserated with her on how scary her situation was, agreed with her that things could go terribly wrong, and generally had a very depressing conversation with her. By the time we ended the conversation, she felt better.

I wished more people had done this with me. By validating her fears I was able to listen to her. She felt heard. It was hard for me to do that when I really wanted to tell her it would all be fine but I gave her what she needed.

What we WISH people would do

1. Take an initiative. Don't ask us what we need…just do.
2. Not forget to extend social invitations to us.
3. Have reasonable expectations of us.
4. Talk about our child with us.
5. Not ignore our loss.
6. Not ask us to look for a silver lining.
7. Visit from time to time.

Cemetery Visits

There is one blogger who frequently writes me and has told me on more than one occasion that she has never visited her baby's grave. I know other women who only go on big occasions, such as the anniversaries of their deaths and their birthdays. In the beginning, we tried to go every week. The fact is, though, it's nearly two hours from us and we have two small children. It's a long, boring day for them and we just can't do that to them that often. Instead, we go for all the major holidays, on his birthday, and on the anniversary of his death.

Some cemeteries have certain regulations that you have to follow. For instance, many don't allow fake flowers. Others don't allow anything like pinwheels or toys or anything that takes up too much room. Our cemetery doesn't care what the heck you do. I like that.

How you choose to decorate your child's grave and how often you visit is entirely up to you. It can be incredibly hard to face your child's gravesite. Others feel like since they can't feel their child there they really don't have a reason to visit it. I can understand this. I have never felt my son's presence in the cemetery but I enjoy being able to do something for him, even if it's just to put flowers on his grave.

Toby's headstone

Celebrations

There are lots of ways to celebrate at your baby's grave. For birthdays many parents have balloon releases and write special messages on their child's balloons as they let them fly into the air. Others buy those large lanterns and light them and allow them to float off.

Actually, that's kind of funny. I am friends with one woman who took the time to write all of our babies' names on the lantern. When they let it loose, though, it got caught in a tree and the tree caught on fire. Sometimes things just don't work out the way you planned and you've got to laugh about them.

On Toby's first birthday we took some sparklers to his grave and stuck them in the ground. My dad lit them and the dry grass around them caught on fire. He was stomping on it in his cowboy boots, trying to put out the flames. I like to think Toby was laughing about that somewhere.

Another friend of mine has a picnic at her child's grave on his birthday. Her living children sing songs to his headstone and write little poems and leave him notes. It's a special day for all of them and she tries to make it fun for them.

Lighting sparklers on his birthday

Kira's experience

(taken from her blog)

Today, at 1:47pm would have been my baby boy's first birthday. I thought I was going to have the strength to go to the cemetery. It rain until early afternoon pouring here in NJ. Jared and I never change from our PJ's we ate sandwiches and had bowls of chocolate ice cream. I cried about 8 times thinking of my baby. We received many messages from many friends. The truth is we are very slowly learning to accept that he is gone. The only comfort we have is that he is not suffering anywhere. But we miss him so very much. I need him so much. The arrival of Kyle in a few weeks, his kicks and non-stop movement made me stop crying today. Jayda and Kylie's smiles and hugs helped us get through this day where we would have been so proud of our baby reaching his first year. I must learn to accept I will never be the same.

I will never be complete.

Ways to celebrate holidays, birthdays, and "Angel Days"

1. Have a party. You don't have to invite anyone but your immediate family if you don't want to. Last year, my 5 year old and I made a chocolate cake and ate it.

2. Make a slide show of your child and watch it together as a family or with friends.

3. Hold a balloon release.

4. Have a service project and get others involved. You could donate food to a food bank, donate items to a NICU, bake cookies for the fire department, or do something for another angel family.

5. Sing songs at their grave and leave little presents.

6. Keep a journal for your child and on every special occasion write a letter to them and let them know how you are feeling.

7. Take your family somewhere special in honor of your child's birthday.

8. Plant a tree or flower in honor of your child.

9. Create a work of art in your child's honor and display it in your home.

10. Buy an item that would be appropriate for his age and donate it to a local children's hospital.

11. Hold a mass or other religious ritual in your house.

If you don't go...

If you don't enjoy going to the cemetery, can't go, or your child isn't buried then there are still some things you can do. Some parents create a special spot in their house and make a kind of memorial to their child. Here, they light candles and place mementos and even fresh flowers, like you might at a graveside. This might be based around their picture, urn, or other item of significance.

You can also create a special place in your yard for your child. A butterfly bush or bench or rose garden...a rock garden...whatever you want, really. This can be your special place to connect with your child and "leave" them things from time to time.

Don't ever let anyone try to make you feel guilty for not visiting your child's grave. On the other hand, if you do visit their grave often then don't let anyone try to make you feel guilty for doing so. You do what you need to do to stay as relatively sane as possible.

The back of Toby's grave

Kira's experience

We are finally having the headstone put in Jayden's burial site. I was there today for the first time since we bury him. It felt like the coldest place in the planet. It is a very peaceful place. Surrounded by beautiful trees. But the silence and the shivering feeling breaks your heart.

I felt my heart racing, panic, so much pain. My knees kept bending my stomach hurt so much and the tears wouldn't stop. It feels like it was just yesterday and it's been 14 months and 10 days since our baby took his last breath. It's so painful to know this is the last time we would buy something for our baby. This is our last gift. This is it. Sometimes it doesn't feel like it happen, sometimes it's so real and sometimes the routine and time just keep you going like you are walking dead. Jared had been there many times. I just never got myself to go. Cemeteries have always frightened me.

The 6ᵗʰ Month Meltdown

Unfortunately, at about the same time that your friends and family seem to think that you should be "doing better" is about the same time that things start getting really, really awful. I call this the "6ᵗʰ month meltdown."

I honestly thought I was making it up until I met other infant loss parents who said the same thing happened to them. I don't know what it is really. It probably has something to do with the fact that we're kind of numb and have a huge rush of adrenalin in the first few months. And, of course, we're more or less surrounded by people who want to do things for us in the beginning. Eventually, however, all of that tapers off and then we're left to deal with the real grief. Not that the grief before the 6ᵗʰ month wasn't real, but it was raw. Painful. Maddening. This new grief is different. It's dull and it cuts into you like a butter knife.

I figured that as time went on I would feel a lot better. And that was true…eventually. At about six months into it, though, I got hit hard. Toby had missed Halloween and Christmas and the snow and Valentine's Day and I just couldn't get a grip on that.

My friends had scattered to the wind for the most part. There were a few faithful stragglers and I loved them dearly but I couldn't figure out why and how I had managed to run everyone else off. I got very upset one day when a friend I hadn't seen in months grew hostile towards me when I tried to invite her over. I got mad at her, wrote a blog entry about her, and that was the end of that friendship. Then, out of the blue, our two best friends totally deleted and blocked my husband and myself and stopped returning our phone calls. To this day I have no idea what that was about.

I felt like people weren't giving me the benefit of the doubt. I felt like they were too hard on me. I felt worthless. I felt depressed. I felt lonely. I was pregnant and sick and spent much of my time in the hospital. I felt like a horrible parent to my surviving child. I cried because I couldn't fix him a snack or play with him or do anything but lie in bed and watch cartoons with him. I cursed the fact that I was having another baby. And then I cried about that.

This was about the time that we were finally able to order the headstone, too, so that was emotional. I had worn everyone out with my depression and complaining. Nobody wanted to hear about my dead son anymore. Nobody clicked on my blog entries and read them. Other grieving parents seemed to have hundreds of followers and comments and I could pour my heart into an entry and not get a single thing. It made me feel worse. I felt like nobody cared.

I even started getting angry and upset at other grieving parents. One mother I had bonded with online often talked about how nobody was there for her and how she didn't have anyone. Feeling the same way, I finally thought I had found someone who understood. Then, when I discovered that hundreds of people had come to her son's funeral, she had raised thousands and thousands of dollars in charity for him through friends and family, and friends had given her things like a nanny service and massages I got angry. That didn't feel like abandonment to me!

At any rate, I didn't feel like I would ever be happy again. I missed my baby. I didn't want to get out of bed, which was good because most days I couldn't.

The guilt of feeling better

It might sound impossible but some people notice a change for the better at around six months. This actually makes them feel worse. There comes a moment when you start feeling a little more human again and you're not crying every day or diving under the covers or wishing you could go to sleep and not wake up. And while that should be a good thing, often it's not. For some people, it feels like "moving on" and they're afraid that if their grief changes it means they don't love their children as much anymore.

That's a really difficult concept for people who haven't lost children to understand. I think a lot of us have faced it from time to time, though. I know that I have felt guilty for not feeling sad on occasion. And then that's made me depressed. It's a vicious cycle. I've also fought against feeling "good" because I don't want to give the idiots who told me to "get over it" or "move on" the satisfaction of thinking that they were right and I would.

Other people

At around six month it also hit me that other people in my life were moving on and seemingly forgetting about my son. That unnerved me. For many of those folks it was as if he had never even existed. I know that they didn't have to talk about him all the time but at least a mention every now and then would have been nice for me. I had no idea how to deal with that. The world was moving but I wasn't. I still felt like I was in the same place, motionless.

I went around most of the time trying to convince people that I had a right to be sad and that it was okay that I was still grieving. I spent so much energy trying to convince others that I had suffered a great loss and that what I was feeling was normal that I considered making a brochure. Now I feel silly about that. Why did I need to convince them that it was okay that I was grieving? What did their opinion matter? But at the time it was very important to me that they "get it."

Karla's experience

My meltdown happened around the 4-5 month range. This was not only when people seemed to be dropping off the radar and not commenting on my Facebook statuses anymore and just in general seemed to be tired of hearing my heartbreak all the time, but also the time that I got the Medical Examiner's report back. Maybe it was the combination of the two but I felt such immense anger at everything. That I got robbed out of a life with my child, that people were tired of listening to something I would have to feel for the rest of my life, and that final closure of his life never to understand why he left so soon. When I got the results back it was as if it really sunk in that it was over, that there would be no more to learn or hear about him. I was mad and upset that there would be no more answers and that I would have to live with it being a mystery. Up until that point there was hope that I would at least hear a better reason then, I don't know. I got past this point by turning my anger and pain and pointing it in the direction of hope rather than despair and started Empty Arms Foundation in order to help find those answers and stop this mysterious killer.

In the 6th month meltdown you might feel

1. A little easier about performing your normal routines.
2. A deep depression.
3. Anger that other people have seemingly moved on from your child's death.
4. Stress and anxiety at seeing other babies who would have been your child's age.
5. Upset when you watch movies or TV shows with small children.
6. In limbo if you haven't been able to purchase your child's headstone or monument yet.

Kira's experience

(taken from her blog)

6 Months today since Jayden stop breathing while he was taking his nap. My heart still broken today, but the last 2 months have been so hard. I have felt so much pain that for the past week I have been working on being ready for this weekend; I have been gentle, I have been exercising, running mostly and eating comfort dessert and stay away from stupid people who can make painful comments. Now at 14 weeks pregnant I'm terrified for the future of this baby. Last year when I was pregnant at this time I was so excited I had found out it was a boy and I could not be more thrilled and excited since I remembered I wanted so much to have a boy. Today I'm excited but the excitement is so limited because of the fear, because I have to accept that I have taken a risk of losing this baby. I have gotten 3 different opinions with different ME's. I have met with three different pediatricians and still no answer. Still no one has any idea of what happened to my baby. I'm a believer of medicine but it's so painful to not know what happen. And even though everyone says you did everything right I feel I messed up somewhere. If not my baby would be here.

You can't be selfish in grief

The other thing I learned around this time was that you just can't be selfish in grief. You would think that it's the one time that you're really entitled to feel what you want to, act the way you feel like acting, and pretty much find your own way but no...you can't.

The first thing you learn is that you have to be extremely open-minded when it comes to religion. Regardless as to what your own religious beliefs are, you are bound to learn everyone else's take on your tragedy and how it relates in a religious way. You listen to people tell you why the person died, what they are doing now, and why you should be happy that they are "at peace", "no longer suffering", etc. You must smile and nod at these things, even if you don't believe them or agree with them, because to insert your own beliefs at this point would be considered rude and ungrateful for the comfort that the person is trying to provide.

You have to accept the fact that everyone is going to interpret your actions differently. If you cry too much then you're going to get accused of depression, in need of psychiatric help, and possibly put on suicide watch. If you don't cry at all, or at least don't do it in public, then you'll get accused of not caring enough. There doesn't seem to be a happy medium.

There is actually an acceptable time limit regarding how long you are allowed to wallow and complain about your loss. It seems to be around two weeks. After that, everyone else is ready to move on and doesn't want to hear about it anymore. You learn not to talk about your sadness with the majority of people because later it comes back to haunt you when people proclaim that you have "too much drama."

Toby's first bath

Of course, it's a little hurtful when you and your "drama" are placed in the same category as those who complain about their frequent breakups, money troubles, and friend bickering. But soon you figure out that complaining is complaining to some people and they just don't want to hear it.

On the same note, you have to be happy and smiley around a lot of people when you do go out or else you're afraid that you won't get asked out again because you're "too depressing." And when in some situations you do forget yourself and actually talk honestly about how you've been and how sad you are and you DON'T get asked to do anything again you'll spend the next month kicking yourself for opening your mouth.

You're not allowed to have temporary amnesia. I have heard other people say that you don't start feeling real pain until months down the line because in the first few weeks or so you're in shock. I believe this. With that in mind, I remember the day that Toby died down to the last detail, regardless of how "out of it" some people describe me as being that day. However, the next few days are a complete blur. I remember things happening but I couldn't tell you who did them. I have no idea how I got dressed, ate, or when or how I slept. I tried to thank everyone but there are still those who believe they weren't thanked enough. I guess I should have kept a record.

You can't get angry or emotional. Other people can lash out at you but if you try to defend yourself or counter-argue then you're ganged up on. Just because you've just had a tragedy doesn't mean you get any leeway.

You have to reach out to most people yourself. While in the beginning people will make an effort to come around, be supportive, and check on you after a few weeks (or days in some cases) you have to make the phone calls and write the e-mails. Which might be okay if you could even remember what day it was.

You can't talk about your loss to just anyone. There are friends and family who just don't want to hear about it. You learn who not to bring it up in front of and who it's okay to. You end up censoring yourself a lot.

And strangely enough, you find that you end up making other people try to feel better about the situation. When friends, family, and even total strangers talk to you about your situation and start crying or getting upset you turn into the comforter.

This should have been the one time that I was entitled to be off my rocker a little bit. If this isn't the time to go a little crazy and get depressed, then when is?

How Society Treats Us

Before I lost my son I was a family therapist for awhile. This was more like a social worker kind of position and not a counseling one. I vividly recall sitting in a staff meeting at one point and talking about someone who had lost a child to SIDS. The therapist who was going to be working in the family's home was looking for ways to help the woman prevent SIDS from happening to her next child. The general consensus in the room was that she must have done something wrong and hopefully, with our help, it wouldn't happen again.

This would come back to haunt me.

Once the overwhelming grief began to subside a little bit and I ran out of people I knew to piss off, I turned my attention to the rest of the world. What I was reading on messageboards, forums, Facebook statuses, and in newspaper articles infuriated me. I became a one-woman SIDS informational ninja, intent on fighting every single battle I encountered. It was exhausting but I think I might have actually made some sense here and there, although I don't know that I changed anyone's mind.

The fact is, there is so much misinformation out there about SIDS and infant death that it's nearly impossible for people to look at us without suspicion. Take, for instance, some of the signs that you see posted on hospital walls and in doctors' offices. You know, the ones that say "SIDS Prevention" and then lists all the things that you're supposed to do to keep your baby from dying. Just the word "prevention" implies that SIDS can be stopped and, by proxy, implies that we must not have done at least one of those things since we no longer have an infant.

Nobody wants to believe that a baby can just die. It infuriated me after I lost my son and other parents would talk about how they "weren't worried" about their infant. I thought they sure as hell should have been. I mean, I didn't want them to be the paranoid freak I was (okay, maybe I did just a little bit) but it made me mad and hurt my feelings that their blasé attitudes about it somehow seemed to imply that they weren't worried because they wouldn't repeat my mistake...whatever that mistake must have been.

Our friends

Our friends, bless them, probably have no idea what to do with us. If you think about it, we really are kind of hard to deal with. I mean, if they talk to us about our infant then we're liable to break down into tears and become emotional wrecks, whether we're in the car or at the movies. On the other hand, if they don't bring up our infant and our loss then we're just as likely to get angry at them for ignoring our pain.

Some friends dropped us as soon as the grave was covered. They either couldn't, or wouldn't, comfort us and felt like it was safer to just watch us from afar until we were "safe" again.

Other friends got angry almost right away because they didn't like the way that we were dealing with our loss. They were positive that, had they been in our shoes, there was no way they would have been as angry/sad/emotional/crazy. They judged us for the way we handled every single thing and self-righteously threw their noses up in the air as they sailed out of our lives.

Some friends took our pain personally. Sometimes, they took it *too* personally. We ended up having to comfort them for our loss which made us kind of happy in the beginning because we liked having people around who were just as depressed as we were and resentful later on because they barely knew our child and they were taking up too much of our energy.

In the worst situations, our friends made our lives harder. They went beyond not knowing what to say and made complete fools of themselves with their harsh words and judgment and inability to try to understand anything we were going through. Some of those we cut off. Some of those actually cut us off first, which was kind of weird since they were the ones being the assholes to start with.

Then there were the friends who walked that fine middle ground. They ignored our rants and anger filled blog entries and Facebook status updates. They patiently sat with us while we cried and shouted and sometimes stared blankly at the television and didn't talk at all. They continued to visit, to ask us to go to the movies, to send us text messages to see how we

were, and to bring up our child in conversation to prove that
they still thought about them.

Those friends were rare.

Total strangers

Dealing with total strangers is often a mixed bag of nuts. You
never know what you're going to get. You really have no idea
how often children come up in random conversations with
strangers until you have lost one. Suddenly, you are on high
alert, just waiting for that question that you know is going to
come: "How many children do you have?"

How do you answer this? Do you tell them the number
of living children you have? Do you count them all and ignore
the fact that one is gone? Do you give them the whole rundown
on how many living and how many deceased you have? Do you
kind of gauge the situation and see which one you're feeling at
the moment?

In the beginning this can be the most traumatizing
experience you can face. Well, that and going out in public and
running into people who don't know that your child died and
having them ask how your child is. That is worse. Luckily, I

lived in a small town with less than 2,000. We put the word out at a few restaurants and in time everyone knew so I no longer got those questions. They still came up when I ventured outside the county line, though.

Total strangers and partial strangers get a little bit of leeway because you don't know them. That doesn't mean you don't sometimes want to throttle them, though.

Sometimes you find yourself giving medical lectures to random people. You start explaining SIDS or cancer or whatever awful thing took your infant from you and you end up sounding like a medical textbook salesperson.

I know one woman who, when she runs into old friends or strangers, tells them about her blog so that they can read about her feelings. I have stopped doing that. My blog has caused too much trouble. To the people who find it, good luck. I'm not paving the way for them, though.

Our doctors

Nothing sends up the red flags to doctors about a potential paranoid parent than learning that they lost an infant. It was difficult finding good medical care for my children before one died but after losing one it's almost impossible. Nobody wants to take you seriously because they just assume that you're super paranoid and a hypochondriac. (In some rare cases the doctor is actually super concerned about every little thing because you have lost a child but this has not happened to anyone I know, just some I have read about.) Seriously, I have had to fight for every illness my children have suffered through since losing Toby.

I have also had to fight for myself. I ended up having to have brain surgery for what was initially diagnosed as depression and anxiety. (I'll give my doctor that one, because she was a good doctor. And the symptoms did make sense at the time.) In my rainbow pregnancy I had just about everything go wrong that could go wrong and if there hadn't been actual tests to prove it then I am sure I would have been swept right out the door with a pat on the head.

After having my rainbow baby I was still in the hospital when a pediatrician came in to talk to me. I asked her if my baby could be sent home with a monitor since my last baby had died. She started lecturing me. I argued with her. Later, a nurse came in and said that the doctor had called in a social worker for me. The social worker asked if I would like any information on SIDS. "No," I replied. "Would *you* like some?"

That's right. We are often more informed than our doctors. We become experts on the things that killed our children. We suddenly know more than the doctors do. I mean, it makes sense, really. With all the illnesses and medical conditions out there they probably have enough on their plates. Us, on the other hand, we have all the time in the world to study and keep up with the latest research and theories.

Thankfully, I was finally able to find a pediatrician who might think that I am a paranoid freak but at least doesn't treat me like one.

Some mothers have had the exact opposite experience when it comes to healthcare, however. They have actually found that their pediatricians and OBGYNs are more forgiving and patient with them and handle them gently.

The media

Earlier I said that I ended up fighting a lot of online fights for things that had been written about SIDS. Well, I have truly seen it all-from newspaper articles that say there is no such thing as SIDS to forums where the posters ("alpha moms" in most cases) talk about how it's only poor people and uneducated people rolling over on their babies in the middle of the night that causes infant deaths. It actually got to the point where any time someone was saying something incredibly stupid and untrue a friend would send me the link so that I could go give them my two cents. And sometimes I brought friends.

The media likes a good story. They want readers. They are going to write anything that gets attention. Unfortunately, that is often at our expense. In addition, professional and responsible journalism is a dying art form. I have been appalled at the lack of research that many of these stories have going for them as well as the sources that the reporters use to start with. Why not interview a SIDS expert instead of a pediatrician or social worker? And they almost never, ever interview the grieving parents. It seems like nobody wants to hear our stories.

I have followed many SIDS stories online, as well as other types of infant deaths, and it always feels like when they do talk to the parents they have to include something else in the story-like how to "prevent" SIDS or something along those lines. The story has to have a certain call to action to make it interesting. Human interest stories are no longer glamorous.

In one case, though, the media did help a good friend of mine. Her house was broken into and someone actually stole the urn that held her son's ashes. Thanks to some reporters who stayed on top of the story, the urn was recovered (although the crooks had dumped the ashes out). The media treated her well.

Of course, the rest of us wanted to fight the people who had done that to her and hang them up by their toenails but that's a different story.

Things that seem to make us mad at different times (according to my unofficial research)

1. People who try to "fix" us.
2. When someone says to tell them if we need anymore. (When we don't even know what we need ourselves.)
3. People who say, "I know just how you feel."
4. People who try to make sense out of our child's death.
5. Platitudes such as "It's God's will" or "it was for the best."
6. People who ignore our loss.
7. People who press us to talk when we don't want to.
8. When someone says, "You will get over it in time." Nobody ever "gets over it."
9. People who pressure us to be or act happy.
10. When someone tells us that at least we have other children.

11. When someone tries to talk us out of a decision such as having another child or moving.

12. People who have unrealistic expectations as to how we are supposed to feel.

Clinical Things

The experts have to weigh in with their two cents on most everything and grieving is a hot topic in the counseling field. People want to understand us so that they can help us and that would be a good thing. Sometimes, though, it feels like our grieving is under a microscope and when it's studied and talked about too much it almost becomes a clichéd or resorts to stereotyping. Still, it is helpful to understand some of these things.

So what do some of the experts have on us at this point?

Types of grievers

In Dr. Kenneth Doka's book, *Disenfranchised Grief*, he offers a description of different types of grievers. He calls these the Intuitive, Instrumental, and Dissonant grievers. So what does it mean and does it even matter to those of us who are grieving?

The Intuitive Grievers

If you are an Intuitive Griever then you are supposed to feel grief intensely. You might also express your grief by crying and being emotional. Intuitive grievers can express their feelings openly and might even feel physical pain. They're not afraid to talk to other people but might suffer from confusion and find it hard to concentrate.

The Instrumental Griever

The Instrumental Griever tends to feel grief more on the physical level than the emotional one. They might cope with grief by using their problem solving skills and express their grief in active ways or even by using humor. They might try to ignore their feelings in order to cope with their situation and if they do express their feelings they do so in private.

The Dissonant Griever

The Dissonant Griever might handle their grief in a certain way but they don't like the way that they handle it. An Instrumental Griever, for instance, might feel bad that they can't express their feelings more freely. The Dissonant Griever might find grieving the most difficult since they are so conflicted.

Complicated grief

For most people, things do improve a little bit after awhile. They don't necessarily get better but you find different ways to cope and the edge is taken off a little bit. Sometimes, though, even after the passing of time (and we're talking real time here, not six weeks or even six months) things don't get better. In fact, they might even get worse. This is being referred to as complicated grief. In complicated grief the emotions are so painful that you might have trouble living life at all and the pain never dulls.

Infant loss, and child loss in general, is definitely a good setup for complicated grief. What can be worse than losing a child? The experts refer to the grief soon after losing someone as "normal" grief, which I don't really like but I don't come up with these things. The symptoms of normal grief and complicated grief are the same at first. Over time, though, the "normal" symptoms start fading but with complicated grief they don't. It's kind of like being in that worst part of how you felt but on a regular basis.

Some of the signs of complicated grief (as taken from the Mayo Clinic's website) include:

- Extreme focus on the loss and reminders of the loved one
- Intense longing or pining for the deceased
- Problems accepting the death
- Numbness or detachment
- Preoccupation with your sorrow
- Bitterness about your loss
- Inability to enjoy life
- Depression or deep sadness
- Trouble carrying out normal routines
- Withdrawing from social activities
- Feeling that life holds no meaning or purpose
- Irritability or agitation
- Lack of trust in others

It is recommended that if you do suffer from complicated grief then you should see a doctor for help.

I guess the trouble with this is that "time" seems to be subjective. What is "after awhile" anyway? At one point does it go from being normal to complicated grief? I am still under the idea that the worst of the grief doesn't hit until about six months. I think up until then you're kind of in shock, except for maybe those first couple of days when you're in complete terror.

Social Media

Thanks to the new timeline on Facebook I have been able to go back over the years and check out posts, pictures, and statuses long forgotten. It's been eye-opening. I've managed to learn a few things in the process.

Of course, the thing that I really wanted to revisit was the time period surrounding Toby's death. I had sent out text messages and made phone calls while I was in the hospital but I have no record of those. I do have one, however, of my initial status update telling people that he had passed away. I got forty responses (ten responses less than a friend who posted last week that they didn't have their Christmas shopping complete).

Rereading those were very sad. People were shocked. So was I. They all tried to offer words of comfort and I appreciated that at the time. Still do.

It looks like I tried to respond to everyone who sent me individual posts on my wall. I say "looks like" because I don't remember writing any of that.

My FB statuses serve as reminders of that week. I'm glad to have them because that week is a blur to me. I had forgotten, for instance, the friend who came over and fixed dinner one night.

I appreciated the people who had changed their profile pictures to ones that had images of them holding Toby. That was incredibly sweet.

I seemed to be functioning very well. I put together a tribute video, shared funeral arrangements, and posted directions to our house. I wrote individual thank you notes on there and responded to things that people sent me and said to me.

In the days that followed, things got a little...funny. Almost immediately (as in two days later) I had people publicly writing me and telling me to go to therapy. I was polite in my response but, honestly, that wasn't any of their business. Therapy helps some but isn't right for everyone. The fact that, by the date, they were doing this two days after he died was kind of

221

presumptuous. I can't imagine publicly telling someone that they need to go to therapy. Shouldn't that be something between the individual and their doctor or spouse?

I was rereading many of these things for a specific purpose. There were people that totally dropped off the face of the earth weeks and months after Toby died. I never heard from them or saw them again. I have felt hurt about that. A lot. One person said that they were tired of "the drama." It wasn't just that they deleted me, they blocked me completely.

I could kind of understand that. I thought that maybe my posts had been too depressing, too angry, too much…After having so many bad things happen all at once I figure that people just didn't want to deal with me anymore.

I don't think so.

After sitting there for nearly two hours and rereading my statuses from 2010-2011 I was not as negative as I had thought. Yes, there was drama with my brother-in-law (rereading that comment again was enraging-not even a month after Toby's death and he gets on my page and leaves such a hateful thing?) and with my father-in-law and later with Pete's former friend, but most of what I posted about that I left to my blog. I made a comment here and there but they were certainly NOT the majority of posts.

In between talking about being sad and lonely and scared I also talked about funny things that Sam said, fun things that we were doing to celebrate Christmas and other holidays, movies I had just watched...There were many, MANY positive things on my FB account. I would even venture to say that the positive far out-weighed the negative.

And even if it hadn't...did I not deserve a year of feeling crappy? Forget a year...who the hell is putting any time limit on feeling crappy when someone loses a child?

I'll give you an example: on the day that I wrote about Dad's heart attack I posted the following...

Saw Dad today. He looked tired, but good. Pete left his backpack in Ashland and remembered it once we got to Morehead so we had to go back. In retaliation, I made him listen to three hours of Juice Newton and Selena.

In that same week I wrote:

found out that two people changed their profile pictures here on FB because they were afraid that they would make me sad. While not necessary, it was incredibly thoughtful and I am touched.

actually watched "Troll" today-the first time since 1989. I had
forgotten that Noah Hathaway was in it! Feeling slightly dirty and old
now...

Rereading things, I was once again shocked at the things that
people wrote to me. At one point I said I was going to the
cemetery to put flowers on his grave. Someone wrote me and
said that they didn't visit their dad's grave because it was
"stupid and pointless." I also wrote and said that I was making a
scrapbook of cards that people had sent me. The same person
commented and said that they didn't keep the cards they got
when their dad died because it was "stupid." This person later
deleted and blocked ME.

I also love the people that wrote me and apologized for
not visiting or getting in touch me and told me that they had just
been too busy and too tired when they got off work. Later, in the
same thread, I would ask them if they would like to come over
the next day or meet for lunch and they would respond by
telling me that they couldn't because they were driving ten
hours to go to a concert and wouldn't be back for two days.
Awesome.

And then there were the people that used their statuses
to report to their friends about everything they were doing for
me. In turn, they would get thirty replies with pats on their

backs about what a great friend they were being to me. I am highly suspicious of their intentions.

I was afraid that I hadn't been thankful enough, hadn't said enough, hadn't been appreciative enough. I see no signs of that now.

Yet, even in that, I managed to live somewhat of a regular life last year. The fact that many others always wanted me to be positive, wanted me to "get better" and didn't want to hear me talk about Toby because it "might make [me] sad"- I think it was about them. I don't think any of that was about me at all. I think they wanted the worst to pass because it made them uncomfortable to have to deal with it.

And the last thing I learned from my Facebook timeline? That it's been the really random people that stuck in there from the very beginning and didn't judge or criticize or pry…they were just there. Looking back over my posts, their presence was always a good one. And I appreciate that, too.

One friend of mine had to delete her account after her son died. She said that she couldn't stand posting a picture of her son and having someone write, "So sorry for your loss" only to have them turn around and post a status about getting drunk and going out. Other friends have created alter egos that allow them to connect with their infant loss friends and talk with freedom about their deceased children without making anyone they know upset.

The Parallel Universe

Losing your child ends your world as you know it. What continues is almost a parallel universe that is nearly unrecognizable.

Parents that lose children are no longer naïve. We know bad things can happen and we can't take for granted that everything is going to work out fine. I try to be positive when I can but since Toby died it's been very difficult. People will say things to me like, "Oh, I prayed for you to get better soon!" And while I appreciate the sentiment, I also prayed during the entire ambulance ride and when we got to the hospital and bad things still happened. Or when I worry about a future pregnancy and someone says, "Everything will turn out fine!" Yeah, that's what *everyone* said to me last time, and *nothing* turned out fine.

It really warps your sense of reality.

One night I was watching something on television and there was a medical show where the examiner examined the body of an infant that died from SIDS. I shouldn't have watched it, but I did. The autopsy bit was difficult but I couldn't take my eyes away from it. Then I switched over to "Hoarders" and one of the women they were profiling had started hoarding after losing her infant to SIDS. It was a bad night for television.

Sitting with Sam on the couch, watching TV, a diaper commercial came on and they played "Silent Night" while showing images of babies. We played that song at the funeral. I started crying and Sam goes, "Do you miss Baby Brother?" When I said that I did he patted me and said, "Well, he died. But we'll have another Baby Brother. And he'll be for you and for me."

Nothing is ever the same again, not even television.

There are so many things that become hard to deal with after losing your child, even if you didn't have trouble with them before.

One night I read a book that bothered me to no end ("Cujo", if you're interested). I had seen the movie a hundred times but the book's ending was a lot different. (The kid dies.) They described the dead body so well that it really shook me up and then all I could see was Toby's face. Not the *live* Toby, unfortunately, but the face that I saw when I first discovered him. I couldn't shake that for hours and I started understanding why people with PTSD would kill themselves. It's not because you don't want to live, but because you can't get outside of yourself and get beyond something. It kind of takes over.

I think we all have a little something different in the way that his death affected us. With Pete, he thinks everyone is dead. I catch him checking random babies' pulses. I constantly wake up to his fingers on my throat, checking to see if I am alive. He checks Sam several times a night. He says that when he wakes up in the morning, he just assumes that everyone in the house is dead and always feels a cold panic.

For me, it's a clingy sadness/guilt thing. It gives me anxiety attacks. Sam brings me his stuffed animals and refers to them as his "friends" and I feel so sad for him that I start shaking and getting cold and I just want to hide in the closet or somewhere dark and small. (And I'm claustrophobic so this makes no sense.) Or, I start thinking about Sam going to school and being picked on, growing up and moving away, or even just getting hurt and I start crying and shaking and freaking out to the point where if I could take my anxiety medication I would.

Me and Sam

Our other children

When I lost Toby I didn't become childless. I still had a living
child in the home which I actually think makes for a different
situation. If there are "stages" of grief then I believe those of us
with surviving children might have moved through them faster.
I didn't always appreciate that at the time.

Along the way, I have made friends with other mothers
who, in addition to losing their child, were also going through
foreclosures, deaths of parents, life-threatening illnesses, and job
losses. The reality was, life continued to go on around them and
they weren't able to shut down like they wanted to. Like *I*
wanted to. We went immediately from Toby's loss to a
horrendous pregnancy with Iris that could have killed us both.

And, in its own terrible way, that was almost a saving grace for us.

What I *did* learn, though, was that my fear of losing another child would intensify. That fear was not with Iris (my subsequent child), however, it was with Sam. I am always grateful when someone asks me about Sam. In the online bereavement communities I have never identified myself as "Toby's mommy" because Sam was here first and is still here and it always felt disloyal to him.

My fear of losing Sam after Toby died grew unreasonably strong and continues to engulf me today. I talked to another mother about this (she also has a daughter Sam's age) and she said she feels the same way. Her fear of losing a child is *not* over her subsequent infant, but over her eldest-the one that was with her when her infant died.

Sam often sleeps with us. He didn't before Toby died. Iris does not. I check on Sam constantly throughout the day. Sometimes, I cry when he's gone. He spends the night with my mom and Pete and I are up until 2:00 am, sniffling and missing him. I find myself waking up in the night, checking to see if he's breathing. Iris has had to have loads of tests, some of which required her to be sedated. We were worried, but we let them do them. Sam was supposed to get his tonsils out and we wouldn't make the appointment because we didn't want him to go under.

This is all directly related to Toby's death. So to ignore Sam in my grief over Toby is unimaginable.

I have spoken to other bereaved mothers who had surviving children at the time of our infants' deaths and they have all agreed: they might not be the infants we lost or our subsequent children, but they are still our *babies*.

They are the ones who were with us when we went through the unthinkable. They are our little champions. They are the ones we held onto at night and loved when it felt like we had nobody else in the world. They are the ones who watched their siblings die and attended their funerals and learned from an early age that sometimes things won't be okay. We protected them and loved them and made them the centers of our world like we hadn't before. They became even more important to us. Our subsequent children might have offered hope for the future, but our surviving children were some of our only links to the people we were in the past.

They forced us to celebrate holidays we couldn't have done on our own. They made us get out of bed and leave the house and attend birthday parties and hayrides and visits with Santa when all we wanted to do was take Tylenol PM and watch episodes of "The Golden Girls."

They gave us a reason to live.

The thought of something happening to Sam is too much to bear. My Facebook friends know him well. He's the little boy who said he wanted to watch "that movie about American history" and was referring to *Bill and Ted's Excellent Adventure*. He's the little boy who spent all evening wrapping me Christmas presents-some of his toys and a cheese sandwich so that I wouldn't get hungry. He's the little boy who asks me to take him to the flea market (without his sister) so that we can "have some private time." He's the little boy with my facial features who has developed my love of photography and old houses and can sing every Christmas song that comes on the radio.

He's the little boy who said that when he grows up he wants to be a cop so that he can "guard that kindergarten school so that nobody else can get hurt."

Sometimes, I miss him and he's not even gone.

Sam

232

So much is written about the children we lost and the children that followed those we lost. But what about the "other" ones?

Trying to be compassionate

Sometimes we talk about how much more compassionate we feel since losing our children. Other times we talk about how less compassionate we feel and how awful we feel because of it.

A friend recently lost their grandmother. Their grandmother had lived a long life and died from natural causes. The friend was understandably upset. Their FB status, however, garnered more than forty-three sympathetic, some of them poetic and expressing their deepest sympathies in ways that almost made me feel uncomfortable. I left mine but it felt empty on my part. I felt like I was just saying the words. Of course, I didn't want my friend to feel sad, but it was hard for me to feel sad *for* them.

Morally, I feel like since they're a friend I should feel supportive of them during their time of pain. A colder side of me feels like I shouldn't care, especially since this is a person who has never reached out to me. A different side of me sometimes doesn't feel anything at all. I do think that part of this process involves a certain amount of numbing.

Sometimes I think that my tolerance is a lot lower than it used to be in terms of sadness. In other ways, I feel like it's higher.

It makes me feel like I'm a bad person. Every once in awhile, though, I'll be feeling something crappy and I'll think I'm being terrible but then I'll read someone else's blog and they'll take the words right out my mouth. Then, I'll at least feel less alone.

Ellen's experience

After my child died people seemed to expect me to be a lot more sympathetic. I wasn't. When I was feeling particularly heartless and someone told me that their grandmother had passed away or that their mother'd had a stroke or something I felt bad for them but my first thought was always something like, "Well, they were old" or "At least he/she is still alive!" I know that sounds horrible but after losing my child it was just really hard to feel bad for someone whose loss didn't seem as significant as mine. I tried to remind myself that just because our pain wasn't similar didn't mean that the person wasn't still hurting but every time a friend would talk about their kid having the

flu or strep throat or something like that I feel empty. As long as they
weren't dead or fighting some terminal illness it just didn't seem that
bad to me.

Now that some time has passed by I am starting to feel more
sympathetic again. In the beginning, though, it was really hard. If my
own child got sick then I freaked out. If someone else's did, though, I
just kind of shrugged it off. I hated being that person, but that's just the
way I felt.

The subsequent child paradox

I was watching my kids play together recently and my mom
asked me if I ever thought what it would be like to have all three
of them running around. This poses an interesting question
because, the fact is, I would have never had all three running
around together.

Many people knew that they were going to have more
children, even before they lost their infant. We were not one of
those people. Toby was a surprise and we worried about him
coming along, thinking that there was almost too much of an age
gap between him and Sam (three years). We were glad that he
came when he did, though.

Due to the complications that I had in his pregnancy and the problems that I had with my reproductive system, there were never any plans to have anymore after Toby. In fact, we had scheduled my hysterectomy shortly after his birth. I was supposed to have it done the week that we buried him. If Toby had died a week later, there wouldn't have been an Iris. If Toby had lived, there wouldn't be an Iris.

Clearly, I would not trade one child for the other. It's kind of maddening to think that without Toby dying there wouldn't be an Iris, though. Of course, we wouldn't have known about her so we wouldn't have known what we were missing, either.

Pregnant with Toby

One of the reasons that the phrase "You can always have another one" is bothersome is that the person saying it does *not* know that the person to whom they are speaking can have another one.

Sometimes it feels like our lives are split in two, like in parallel universes. There's the one with Sam and Toby and then there's the one with Sam and Iris. They're two totally separate lives that will never overlap.

I ended up having a hysterectomy shortly after Iris was born so there won't be any more children for us.

Pregnant with Iris

But you're doing so well!

A friend posted the following sign on FB: "Don't judge me. You couldn't deal with what I have dealt with." That, combined with the occasional comment along the lines of, "You're doing so well!" after someone finds out we've lost a child got the wheels turning.

For starters, you have no idea what you can handle until it's actually thrown at you. I would never be so ornery or lofty as to think that someone else wouldn't be able to handle my tragedies as well as I have. That attitude wouldn't be any different than the person who thinks they could have handled it better than me and you know how much *that* bugs me. Until you're put in that situation yourself, you have no way of knowing what you're going to do or how you're going to react. No amount of books, movies, song lyrics, or poetry is going to adequately prepare you.

In the beginning, when people told me that I was doing well and that I was really "holding up" it confused me. It made me feel as though I wasn't grieving as I should be. This was especially hurtful when people would say things to me like, "I just couldn't live if something like that happened to me." Like I was failing Toby by not caring enough because I somehow made the choice to live.

My friends and I talk about this a lot. Those comments stung them, too. We are able to function, do the things we need to, and put on pretty good outward appearances. But nobody is around to see us crying ourselves to sleep every night. Sometimes it feels like people say these things to us to get us to agree that we are doing well so that they won't have to deal with us.

The fact is, none of us are doing "well." We are all able to function on various levels but that doesn't mean that we enjoy it. It doesn't mean that it doesn't take a whole lot of energy to be able to do simple things. Yes, we got out and did things after Toby died, but most of that was because we had Sam. It wasn't fair to him to check out like we wanted to.

I think it's wrong to look at another person and feel superior to them in our own grief because they're not showing it as much. We have no idea what the other person is feeling. Even when it comes to blogging, some people blog differently. There are some SIDS blogs out there that feel really positive. But we don't know what that person feels once they turn the computer off. On the flip side, some of us write things that are very

239

depressing and open but that doesn't mean that we don't have moments during the day where we aren't laughing or enjoying ourselves. In fact, I think the yo-yoing is one of the worst parts of grief-you'll feel almost okay one second and be having a complete nervous breakdown the second.

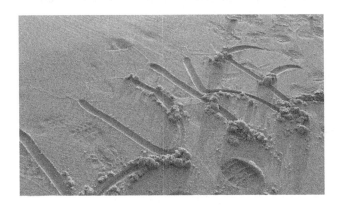

A new normal=a new life

After having such a blow as losing your child you really do have to start over from scratch in a sense. Your relationship dynamics change, your feelings change, the way you approach life in general changes...That's one of the reasons why I think we have so much trouble identifying with others now who have not experienced something of this caliber-we're just not on the same wavelength. We're like moving sidewalks in Vegas-ultimately going in the same direction but on different tracks. And some aren't sidewalks at all-some are escalators. Hell, some are *rollercoasters.*

There have been a few people that ran for the hills after Toby died but there are just as many that we cut out ourselves. Being friends with them was fine when we were different people and had high tolerances and lots of time and energy to cater to their whims and needs. Now, not so much.

I think there comes a point in this aftermath where we have to be gentle and forgiving with ourselves and be like, hey, it's okay to cut ___ out. I don't want to work there anymore, I don't have anything in common with them anymore, I don't enjoy doing that anymore, etc. The more we can do for ourselves and take care of ourselves, the better.

My friend said that he's a different person now and will never be the old one again. I agree. Instead of trying to get back to the old me, I have started trying to move forward with the new one. That might not sound like such a big deal, but it kind of is.

Karla's experience

Kyle's little light will shine on because of what I do and accomplish in his name, not because he is in some mystical land. This focus lifted me from the depths of despair and gave me a direction to go in. Whether religious or not, being able to lift your head up from the darkest moments after child loss begins with how you choose to focus on your future. Dwelling on the "could haves" and should haves will never let you move along in your grief. Although we all have times these thoughts and feelings overwhelm us, it's whether we can stand back up again after they knock us down that matter.

Valerie's experience

One day when my rainbow, Alyssa, was probably about 5 months old the funniest/ sickest sense of humor type of thing happened. I was over at my mom's house and she was asleep in her car seat. I had many tactics to check on her, one being that I would hold this little compact mirror up under her nose and look for the little fog that breath makes. Here's the sickly funny part... I held it up under her little nose and she began to move her head out of irritation. Instead of backing off and being assured that my baby was fine, my obsessed ass followed her attempting to get that little fog I wanted to see. After a split second, I pulled back and my mom and I had the biggest laugh. Maybe even the first real laughter since my loss. That was healing and I did begin to relax a little. Just what I needed to grow through my grief. In fact, I think that the worry I went through with Alyssa has definitely helped me to worry less with Brandon now. I will definitely love and miss Haylie until the day I die, but I do feel like I have arrived at my "new normal" in many ways.

The Rainbow Pregnancy

I would venture to say that at some point all of us have thought about getting pregnant again or have gotten pregnant with a subsequent child. Some of us might have even been considering that the day we buried our infant.

Some people might not understand the immediate need to have another baby. I don't think it's that strange. After all, your body and mind are already convinced that you have an infant. Your breasts might be full of milk, your ears tuned into the sound of tiny cries, and your sleep still on your baby's schedule. Biologically, you have a baby you need to take care of. Only thing is, your baby is not there. I honestly believe that your body reacts to this by saying, "Hey, okay, then we need to fix this! Get me another child!" It's not a mean thought, it doesn't mean you want to "replace" the child you just lost…it's just a biological reaction.

Some people, too, realize that they just aren't ready to stop having children. I know many parents who planned on having a whole houseful. I know others who weren't going to have anymore (like us) but once they did they loved having that large family and now they don't want to give that feeling up. We realized right away that we liked our child having a sibling. We didn't think we would.

Here's a secret I am going to share about having a subsequent child or a "rainbow" baby: whatever your reason is for getting pregnant again, it's nobody's business.

Kira's experience
(taken from her blog)

Tomorrow my baby Jayden would have been 9 months old. I miss him so very much. Every single day I grieve the fact that he is gone. Today at 20 weeks pregnant we found out we are having his baby brother. I broke down and started crying because it's terrifying. It's so scary to think that we may lose this baby too. We have our two older girls and for some reason I thought that having another girl will be easier since our girls are alive and our son is gone. The technician looked at me and

said, "Well, God may be giving you a son back" and I'm due on
February 6th the day we lost our baby. We know God had nothing to
do with Jayden been gone. We also know that God will give him back to
us one day and it's the only thing that helps today. It's not that I'm
strong-I have no choice. I must keep going my girls, my husband and
now our Baby boy that is growing inside my belly need me so much.
Jayden will mean everything to me always. And his little brother will
know how his mommy fell in love once again. We are happy but
terrified at the same time.

Other people's opinions

When you decide to get pregnant again you will find that
everyone has an opinion about it. Some will be overjoyed
because they will be under the impression that this will "fix" you
and make you "happy" again. Others will think you're making a
terrible mistake and should wait. Some will think you're out of
your ever loving mind. And then you'll have a few who think
it's a fantastic idea and are ready to start shopping for baby
clothes with you.

I was reading one grief manual and it was geared
towards what you could do for someone who is grieving. It said
that you should try to talk the grieving person out of making

any "big decisions." I disagree. I don't think this is being a friend. Yes, their decisions might not make sense to you but unless it involves something life threatening the REAL job of a friend is to be supportive. They should grit their teeth and bear it.

The only two people whose opinions really matter where this is concerned are your partner and your doctor. Your doctor might have some concerns if your last pregnancy was complicated or recent. And your partner should always have input. If you have older children then their ideas might be included, too. Our son was three at the time of his brother's death so we didn't really talk to him about our subsequent pregnancy. To him, babies represented death and horror and funerals so we tried to keep the news to a minimum. Even after his sister arrived he still wasn't convinced that she was here to stay.

One of our "friends" told us that we needed to "take some time" and "focus on [our living son]" and a bunch of other things. I am glad we didn't listen to him.

Pregnant with Iris

When only one is ready

Sometimes only one person in the partnership wants to have another baby. This can feel heartbreaking to the other. There are lots of reasons why one parent might not want to try to have another child. The idea of losing a second child is unbearable. Perhaps the last pregnancy was difficult and they just don't want to go through that again. Or, maybe they simply don't want another disruption because they are starting to feel some sense of normalcy. All of these are natural reactions.

Time is usually the best balm for this. Pushing your partner is definitely not going to work. They'll feel resentful and you'll feel bad and then it will be a mess. Even if you're so ready you are already buying baby clothes you need to give it a little bit of time. If, then, your partner is still isn't on board then you might want to try talking to a third party, such as a doctor or counselor. This can be a very delicate time and a professional outsider mediating (not a friend or family member) might be needed.

Things to remember about a subsequent pregnancy

1. You won't have a baby right away. It will still take the normal forty weeks or so to arrive. This can be hard when you want one NOW.
2. You might have trouble conceiving. Depression and stress don't make an ideal environment in your womb.
3. Everyone will have an opinion about it.
4. You might have the opposite gender of what you had the last time. This can be upsetting.
5. You might have the same gender you had the last time. This can be upsetting.

6. If you get pregnant right away your baby might be born on the same day as the child you just lost. This can be disconcerting.
7. Pregnancies that are close together can be difficult on the body.
8. There is research that shows that SIDS *might* increase with each subsequent child. The research is not updated, but it is out there.
9. A subsequent pregnancy might be very hard on you emotionally. Some parents find that they can't bond with the child in-utero.
10. A subsequent pregnancy might actually help the grieving process as it gives you something joyful to look forward to.
11. You might not find the support from friends and family you expected to have.
12. People might be overwhelmingly supportive.

My experience

My rainbow pregnancy was not a pleasant experience. We got pregnant on purpose and in hindsight I honestly believe it was the best decision we made. The pregnancy itself, however, was fraught with pain, terror, and depression.

For starters, it was a hard pregnancy. I had every single complication that could happen: preeclampsia, intrauterine growth restriction, gestational diabetes, partial placental abruption, subchorionic hematoma, hyperemesis gravidarum...

These things, coupled on top of the natural fear of having another baby and losing that one as well, were almost too much to take. I considered abortion at one point. I considered adoption at one point. I even thought about killing myself. I talked about it with fellow SIDS mothers who were pregnant at the time and was slightly relieved, and concerned for them, to find that these feelings were shared.

I could NOT share any of this with most of my "normal" friends. They were already worn out from my depression, anxiety, and what they perceived as constant drama and complaining. If they had *really* known how I felt I probably would have been committed. Here is a blog entry toward the end of my pregnancy that I only shared with fellow bereaved mothers:

I am a terrible, terrible person. I spent the day at the hospital today. I'm still measuring less than what I should be at this stage. I did get to see Iris' hair on the ultrasound and she sucked her thumb and waved and even opened her eyes. They think I'm going to be okay and can at least make it to 32 weeks which is just a week and a half away.

All of this should make me happy. And it does. And yet…

There are days when I not only do not want to be pregnant but I am not even sure that I want this baby. I fell horrible about this. I read what other mothers write on the SIDS board about wanting to have another baby and get pregnant again and I was definitely with them right after I lost Toby. I wanted to get pregnant so bad. But now that I am…I just can't bond with her. I can't associate the life that is inside of me with a real baby. I did NOT have this problem with my other two. Sam and I bonded the minute I found out that I was pregnant and that bond is still very strong. My husband is jealous. With Toby, it took a little longer. With Iris, though…I don't know.

I don't know if it's because I've been so sick this pregnancy and haven't been able to enjoy it, because I'm scared of SIDS again, or if it's depression and the PTSD acting up. I just don't know what to do.

I have briefly talked to my husband about this and he feels the same
way. He's excited on a superficial level because it's a girl and he loves
babies but he isn't sure that he wants to be a father again, either.

I want to be honest but at the same time I am going to sound
totally selfish…I like where we are right now as far as our family life
goes. (Everything else is going to hell in a hand basket, but we still
have fun as a family.) I love the relationship I have with Sam and I feel
that things are finally starting to calm down after Toby's death. Sam is
no longer afraid all the time and wearing his cardigans, we aren't
waking up every 10 minutes to check to see if he is breathing (we've
moved it up to at least every 30 minutes), he's finally sleeping through
the night, and I'm working again with gusto that I haven't had in 9
months.

I even briefly thought about adoption today. I can't do that,
though. I would worry about her too much. All my life I have wanted a
little girl and it's a miracle that I am having one. I am the first person
in my generation (and there are 37 of us) to have a girl. I saved some of
my old stuffed animals for her and toys since I was a kid, preparing for
the day that I hoped to have a daughter. And now I feel so indifferent
and instead just feel really clingy to Sam.

There's no way I could talk to anyone about this, other than
my husband and the people on here. My friends write me and say
things like, "Only 8 more weeks!" and such and that just sends
terrifying chills through me.

Anyway, I'm just worried. When I talked to my husband about it he said that he felt this way with both of our kids but that once they got here and he met them he couldn't have loved them anymore. He said that maybe I'm just taking the male side this time, the whole "men become a father when they see their baby" thing. I hope he's right.

I will say this, however. Although it took me several weeks to really bond with her, having Iris was the best thing I did. She is a complete joy and totally turned my grieving around. I can't imagine life without her. I look back on that past blog entry with shame and then try to tell myself that it's okay, that it was just how I was feeling at the time and we can't control our feelings. I wished I didn't have them, but I can't take them back. There has never been a day of regret since she was born, though. She is a goddess.

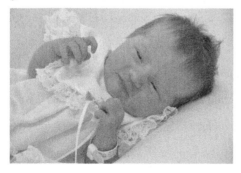

Iris

What did we do differently

When Iris was about a year old I sat down and wrote a blog entry about the approach we took to Iris and her birth. Here is that entry:

When I was pregnant with Iris, we decided that this time we would go by the book. We would follow all the rules and precautions and be pretty much prefect parents. If Iris died of SIDS, it would be because some energy force was messing with us-NOT because we did or did not do something that could have prevented it.

So how did we fare?

Well, most of that went flying out the window when she got here.

Babies are different. What Sam liked, Toby didn't like. What Toby didn't like, Iris loved.

Iris does not like to be held like most babies. I wanted to hold her a lot. She didn't want anything to do with it. Sam? You literally could *not* put him down. Toby loved to cuddle so you didn't *want* to put him down. I figured I would hold Iris all the time and be afraid to lay her down. Nope. She screamed until I let her go.

Iris can put herself to sleep. She demands to be left alone.

Iris started sleeping in her baby bed when she was ten months old. Before that, she slept on the couch with her foot propped on me, her favorite blanket brought up to her chin and her head propped on a pillow.

With her reflux, she has to have her head propped up. Without it, she chokes. Without her blanket, she doesn't sleep.

Because of Toby and the SIDS death we made a deal that wouldn't work for other parents: we decided that for the first year of Iris' life we would stay up with her all night. So we did. I stayed up all night with her and worked. I literally sat at her feet until 6:00 am. At that time I went to bed and my husband took over until he had to go to work, usually around 2:00 pm. We did this for over a year.

Iris also likes to sleep on her stomach. So, we let her. No back sleeping for her. I figured I would be dead set against her sleeping on anything but flat on her back. But after months of fighting with her, and months of doing my own research and reading the real statistics about back sleeping, we let her go.

We also thought we would be religious about using the Snuza. We did buy one but after three months the battery quit working. We never got a new one. The Snuza did help us and give us some peace of mind, but since someone was up with her 24/7 anyway, a monitor didn't seem that necessary. More than once it almost made me wreck as I drove down the road with her and it slipped and went off, sending me into a panic.

Iris could care less about using a pacifier, too. Sam HAD to have his. Luckily, he gave it up at 1 year so we didn't have to fight him for it but he couldn't sleep without it before then. Toby was hit and miss. Iris forgets she has one. She does like to stick it in *our* mouths, though. That's the most use she gets out of it.

We don't use a fan.

I did not breastfeed. I chose not to.

I thought that I would get tests run on Iris but none of the doctors would do them. Well, until she failed her newborn screening and they had to. She didn't get any special treatment just because her sibling died of SIDS.

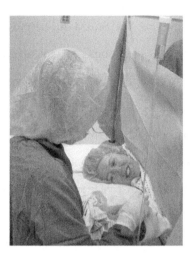

Meeting Iris

We followed all of the "rules" with Toby and he still died. He had his own cradle and crib, used a pacifier, had a fan in his room, didn't have blankets or pillows, slept on his back, and did all of those other things that the guidelines tell us to do. I had good prenatal care, did not smoke, did not do drugs, and provided a healthy environment and womb for him.

Knowing that I did those things, but that he died anyway, does not lessen the guilt or make me feel any better.

When I was pregnant with Iris, planning all the things that we were going to do and things that we could do to make her safe helped ease the stress of the pregnancy and took some of the pressure off. So it definitely had its place. Once she got here, though, the reality of having her here coupled with her own unique personality made those decisions more difficult.

257

Valerie's experience

My first subsequent was planned almost immediately. I had an IUD put in like a week before our loss and knew I wanted it out ASAP. Haylie and Alyssa's birthdays are exactly one year and five months apart! I remember my doctor asking if I was ready for the removal and pregnancy so soon. I told her that this hurt is never going to go away and how I needed to fill my arms again. The way I felt initially was a relief that I had something to keep me going, but as it dragged on, I grew even more depressed. I had a step daughter that I stayed at home with all of the time. She was acting out as an older sibling might do with such grief. When my husband would get home from work they would appear to be just fine though and I was very jealous that he still had someone, but my first child was gone. Resentments were growing rapidly towards her and everyone else, including my unborn child. I wished everyday that I could just have my Haylie back inside of me. So no real bonding with pregnancy happened. When it was closer to time for the sex to be determined, I wished very badly that the baby would be a boy just to be completely different (since I knew I couldn't have my wish for Haylie to come back). I was afraid that if it was a girl, there'd be similarities that would be painful. Needless to say, none of my wishes were granted. When Alyssa got here, she was loved to pieces anyway! She was monitored heavily and it's a wonder anyone got sleep that first year. I poked and I prodded and used an "Angel Care Monitor". It's also a wonder I never got into a car accident. I had one of those mirrors you stick in the back window, adjusted so that I could watch her through my rear view mirror. Now with Brandon (my newest/ only boy/ and last)... He was totally unplanned. I bonded immediately, practically at conception. I didn't care if he was a boy or girl. The pregnancy went well and I'm able to enjoy him with less fear.

Making a plan

One thing that I believe is very helpful during a subsequent pregnancy is to make a plan before the baby is born. Once the baby arrives it's going to be very hectic and you have no idea how you are going to feel. A plan can help take that pressure off.

Here is what we did to alleviate our anxiety. I am not saying that it will work for you, but we planned it out ahead of time, stuck to it, and it worked...

We ordered a Snuza from Europe. This is a small device that clips onto the baby's diaper. When the baby goes for several seconds without breathing the Snuza vibrates and gently wakes the baby up. If several more seconds elapse, the Snuza sends off an alarm. In a true SIDS case the baby cannot be saved. We knew that. We also knew, however, that we could not wake up and find another deceased child. If my baby was going to die then I wanted to be holding him or her while she did. I wanted to be there. That was the peace of mind the Snuza offered me.

Other ideas, though, include:

1. Ask someone to come and help you for the first couple of weeks.
2. Prepare meals in advance and freeze them or use a meal delivery service at first.
3. Place the baby's crib or cradle in your bedroom for as long as you feel comfortable.
4. Talk to your hospital and pediatrician about using a sleep apnea monitor for the first couple of months.
5. Don't get all of your child's vaccinations at once. Space them out to see how your infant reacts to them. It means more trips to the doctor but might make you feel more comfortable.
6. Talk to your job about taking extra time off or telecommuting for awhile so that you don't have to enroll your infant in daycare right away, if that makes you feel more comfortable.

7. Or...enroll your infant in daycare. Some parents find that with subsequent pregnancies they are so terrified of something happening that they can't sleep. You might actually need that help in the first few months.
8. Talk to your doctor about medication for anxiety and depression.
9. Work out a schedule with your partner regarding nighttime feedings. Stick to it.

Bonding

Some women have had trouble bonding with their subsequent pregnancies. As previously mentioned, you know I did. That is not unusual. Your natural fear of losing another one coupled with your grief and anxiety is enough to make anyone aloof. Some people say that all of this changes the minute you see your baby in person. For some people that might actually happen. For others, it might not. It might take longer.

I would say to be easy on yourself. Don't push yourself to feel something you don't. Instead, focus on your health and the baby's health and getting to know your child. The rest should follow. If it doesn't follow then you might want to talk to someone about it. Counselors and drugs (the legal kind) are there for a reason. Don't be afraid to use them.

People have different ways of bonding. I did it by shopping. I know that sounds funny but the best way to bond with my daughter was by buying her stuff. Whenever I was able to get out of the hospital or bed I was at the store or on Macy's website. I adored buying her little frilly dresses and shoes and matching underwear. It was the only way I felt close to her. Other people thought it was ridiculous. It made me feel normal.

We spent an outrageous amount of money on her nursery furniture. People also criticized us for that. I reasoned it with the fact that the last thing I had bought for my baby was a casket. I was due something fun.

We also made a lot of her things as well. We made her bassinette and some of her bedding for her cradle. (We had a bassinette, a cradle, and a baby bed.) I made her wall hanging out of an old sheet and old window. My husband and I embroidered a lot, too, especially during doctors' visits.

10 tips to help you get pregnant faster

1. Start taking prenatal vitamins now. (Okay, this won't help you get pregnant faster but it will be helpful anyway.)

2. Keep track of your periods using a calendar and an online resource which can help you track your days of ovulation.

3. Have sex whenever you can. Seriously. Not just when you are ovulating.

4. Practice some stress relieving techniques. Meditate, journal, sing, draw, whatever...

5. Ask your doctor for an exam to make sure everything looks good. I didn't ovulate for the first few months after Toby died.

6. If it doesn't look good don't be afraid to ask for something that might encourage ovulation and fertility.

7. Buy an ovulation kit from the drugstore.

8. Try to limit heavy smoking and drinking.

9. Get away for a weekend. A weekend adventure can help relieve stress and your body tends to want to conceive when you're feeling relaxed and not so focused on getting pregnant.

10. Lose any excess weight by getting regular exercise and focusing on healthy food choices.

Iris

For what it's worth, I didn't care for the phrase "rainbow baby" because I felt like it was putting too much pressure on the sub baby to brighten us up. I almost never used that term. Iris herself was named after the Americana singer Iris Dement. It wasn't until after she was about three months old that I discovered that "Iris" meant "rainbow." Guess the joke was on me.

Iris

Letting it Out

Sometimes, you just need to let it all out. Despite the fact that I wrote about my feelings in my blog I really felt like I was holding back. In hindsight, I kind of was. I was being very passive aggressive. Rather than confronting the people who were making my life miserable, I wrote about them.

Then, one day when I was feeling at the end of my rope, I discovered a thread on the message board of the online support group that I belong to called the "Bite Me" thread. It was a place for other parents of SIDS babies to vent their frustrations. Some of them were funny, in a sad sort of way. Some of them made me angry. (Not at the poster, but at the people that they are venting at.) But most of them sounded familiar. Finally, *finally* I had people who understood me. And I finally gave myself permission to really, *really* be angry.

I can't share any of those, of course, because they're private, but I added my own two cents and thought I would expand on it. So as not to leave it too negative, though, I thought

I would also end with a "thank you" segment because I think in the long run there really has been more positive than negative. So, here goes…

(And I completely encourage you to do the same.)

To the person who said "at least he was just a baby so it's not like you had a long time to get attached to him", BITE ME.

To the people who get on my blog and read it, not because they care but because they have some sort of sick fascination with me and my grief, BITE ME.

To the people who should have been supportive but instead just caused more grief, BITE ME.

To the people who didn't hesitate to jump onto me whenever I tried to defend myself and my family yet made excuses for the person doing the attacking, BITE ME.

To the people who give me laundry lists as to why they don't call/come around/write, BITE ME.

To the person who said that God is just "testing" me, BITE ME.

266

To the people who don't contact me just to talk, see how I'm doing, or hang out, yet persist to give me medical advice and add their two cents as far as my healthcare is concerned, BITE ME.

To the people who act like Toby never existed, BITE ME.

To the people who claim to miss him, yet never met him, BITE ME.

To the people who say that they don't worry about SIDS because they "follow all the precautions", BITE ME.

To the "family member," and I use that term loosely, who continues to send hateful e-mails and text messages, making things just a little bit worse every day, BITE ME.

To the people who said, "Let me know if you need anything" and then when I asked for something said "no", BITE ME.

To the person who ridiculed me for visiting his grave, keeping nice letters that people wrote me, and other things that make me happy, BITE ME.

To the person who wrote me a cheery "Hope you're doing well!" e-mail four months after he died (without contacting me at all any time in between), BITE ME.

To my "best friend" who hasn't seen Sam since he was seven months old, never met Toby, and didn't even come to the visitation or funeral, BITE ME.

To the people who brag to others about everything they have done for me, BITE ME.

To the "friends" who supposedly came here with "unconditional love" and then placed conditions on everything we did or said, BITE ME.

And now, for the thank you part...

To my friend who, when everyone else said I would be "fine", urged me to go to the ER because I probably had preeclampsia, THANK YOU. She was right and if we hadn't been vigilant, he might not have survived his traumatic birth.

To the paramedics who valiantly turned on the sirens and worked on him all the way to the hospital, even though it was obvious that he was gone, THANK YOU.

To the nurse who sat in the room with me until Mom and Pete got there and cried, THANK YOU.

To the staff at the hospital that left us alone with him for hours, THANK YOU.

To the woman who came up to me in the lobby and hugged me and prayed, THANK YOU.

To the friend who sang the songs at the funeral even though he had just learned them the day before, THANK YOU.

To the funeral home who only charged us their overhead costs, THANK YOU.

To my Aunt Fran and Uncle Ray who drove thirty-two hours to be with us, after just making the drive the week before, THANK YOU.

To the friends that took a week out of their lives and practically moved in with us to make sure that we had food, groceries, and clean bathrooms, THANK YOU.

To the people at the Gathering, many of whom we had only met once before, who sent cards, messages, and donations, THANK YOU.

To the friends who drove a long way to come to the visitation, THANK YOU.

To the friends, family members, and total strangers who sent monetary donations for his funeral and tombstone, THANK YOU.

To the friend who held a yard sale to raise money for us and then took me to get my hair done, THANK YOU.

To the B&B who gave me two free nights after Toby died so that I could recuperate, THANK YOU.

To all the people who got up and spoke at his funeral, THANK YOU.

To the random people who find my blog and send me nice messages, THANK YOU.

Things Not to Say or Do to a Grieving Parent

Some of these things might change. I know that, for me, things that I was sensitive to in the first few months were not the same as they were a year later. If you don't know what to say, a simple "I'm sorry" is always good. When a parent loses a child, you can't fix it for them. What you CAN do, however, is support them, be there for them, and listen.

DON'T ignore the child's death. Talking about other things in an attempt to make the parent "happier" might likely have the opposite effect.

DON'T change the subject when they mention their child. If they bring the child up themselves, chances are they want to talk about them.

DON'T tell them what they should feel or do. Even if you've lost a child before, all experiences are different.

DON'T avoid the parents because you feel uncomfortable. Being avoided can make the parent feel as though they and their child have been forgotten.

DON'T let your friends, family or co-workers grieve by themselves. Grief is already isolating in its own way.

DON'T make any comments which in any way suggest that their loss was their fault.

DON'T point out that at least they have their other children. (Yep, good thing I have that back-up child!)

DON'T say "Your loved one is waiting for you over there," "God wanted him," "It was God's will," or "God knows best." (Just try to convince a grieving parent that someone else knows what is best for their child. It might comfort YOU but that doesn't mean it comforts the other person.)

DON'T bring up a religious reference at all unless you know the parents' religious orientation. Because the thought of the child being in Heaven is comforting to you doesn't mean that it will be for the parents, especially if they are atheist or have other beliefs.

DON'T say "you can always have another child." (Children are not replaceable and what if the person can't?)

DON'T reference the child's age as a positive attribute of the death. (My child was 7 weeks old. Although I didn't know him for as long as someone who lost a 16 year old knew their child, I still knew everything about him and loved him. Saying "at least he was just a baby" is not helpful. It's actually cruel.)

DON'T say "you should be coping or feeling better by now" or anything else which may seem judgmental about their progress in grieving. (How do you know when they should be feeling better? Grief never goes away. This also puts a tremendous amount of pressure on the parent who might feel as though they are already trying hard enough as it is.)

DON'T say that you know how they feel (unless you've

experienced their loss yourself you probably don't know how they feel. Even if you HAVE experienced a similar loss, it's a pretty individual journey.)

DON'T suggest that they should be grateful for their other children. (Grief over the loss of one child does not discount the parents' love and appreciation of their living children.)

DON'T tell them not to cry. (Crying helps some people. It's better to cry than to bottle up emotions.)

DON'T tell them what they should feel or do. (This includes going to therapy. Not everyone does well in therapy, can afford therapy, or wants to go. It's a personal decision.)

DON'T try to find something positive (e.g. a moral lesson, closer family ties, etc.) about the loss. (There is NOTHING positive about losing a child. Period.)

DON'T allow your own fears to prevent you from offering support to the bereaved. (Being around grieving people can be awkward and scary for you. But not half as scary and sad as it is for the person who is grieving.)

DON'T say, "If you need anything call me" because the bereaved don't always know how to call and ask for your support. (And will probably immediately forget that you said that.)

DON'T think that good news (family wedding, pregnancy, job promotion, etc.) cancels out grief. (Yes, happy things do still happen to us and around us. That doesn't mean we are "cured.")

DON'T have expectations for what bereaved parents should or should not be doing at different times in their grief. (For some people simply getting out of bed and getting dressed is a huge accomplishment. They will do more when they are able to.)

DON'T force bereaved people to talk about their loss. They will engage you when the time is right.

DON'T expect grieving parents to be strong and don't compliment them if they seem to be strong. (This makes us place unreasonable expectations on ourselves.)

DON'T say "I couldn't go on if something happened to my child." (Although you might think this is a compliment to the person's inner strength, sometimes it makes the parent feel as though their love for their child is less than what yours is for your own child, simply because they are breathing.)

DON'T assume that when a grieving parent is laughing, they are over anything or grieving any less.

DON'T think that children are too young to appreciate loss or death. (But please talk to your own children about the appropriateness of bringing up the loss around our children or ourselves.)

DON'T talk about the person's feelings or grief publicly with your blog or social media statuses. (It's highly inappropriate to write a status talking about how your friend is feeling suicidal or to write in detail about how your friend is handling their grieving process.)

DON'T compare their loss to a loss you've had. At least, don't do it out loud to them. Losing your dog/grandma/uncle/cat was undoubtedly sad. But it's not the same.

DON'T complain about your living children. (Eventually, you and your friend/family member/co-worker might get back to a point where you can talk about how ornery your child is being and the other person won't be sensitive to it. For awhile, however, this is something you should avoid.)

DON'T question their decisions. (If they want to have another baby right away, your job is to verbally support them, even if you don't understand it. Unless it will physically harm them or possibly have them arrested, just try to go along with it.)

Things I Have Learned Since Losing My Son

1. It's possible to go an entire week and not remember anything that you did.
2. You can feel sad and not actually cry.
3. The things that you cry over are not always the things that you're sad about.
4. Medicine numbs nothing, but it can make you sleep.
5. Nobody has any idea of what to say to you.
6. You don't have any idea of what you want someone to say to you.
7. Despite what they say, nobody really understands.
8. Grief makes people uncomfortable.
9. There are no manuals on how to deal with the loss of a child and all of the advice books in the world do little to help.
10. Grief does not "go away." It changes and dulls.
11. You can actually forget what a person felt like and looked like.
12. People will say, "Let me know if you need anything" but they don't always mean it.
13. Even your best friends can disappear.

14. People are sympathetic and nurturing for about a week and then seem to vanish off the face of the earth and you're left all alone.

15. Real pain doesn't actually set in until months later.

16. People can be mean and cruel even when you're going through your worst times.

17. You can still laugh even on days that you feel like crap.

18. Sometimes the good memories hurt worse than the bad ones.

19. There are some places you will never be able to visit again because the reminders are too painful.

20. People will pass off a lot of things that you do as you "grieving", even when they were things that you did before your loss.

21. Finding answers might not change the outcome, but they can make you feel better.

22. That "what ifs" will drive you crazy.

23. People will come up with a thousand reasons as to why they haven't called, visited, written, or been in touch with you but the fact is, you're still alone regardless as to how good their excuses are.

24. The person might be gone, but everything else is still the same and that's not always comforting.

25. You're no longer innocent when it comes to fearing the worst for your other children.

26. You can feel anger when someone complains about their child being away or being sick-at least they're still alive.

27. And then you feel guilty for thinking those things.

28. Sometimes, you have a good day and then you feel guilty about that, too.

29. When people tell you not to do something (cry, talk about your loss, be angry, or whatever) it's usually because it makes them feel uncomfortable.

30. You can cut off friends and family members without a second thought because since you've lost your child losing someone you barely talk to doesn't seem as traumatic as it might have once felt.

31. Nobody grieves in the same way.

32. Everyone wants to tell you how hard it's been on them since your child died.

33. There are people who think that your loss doesn't matter as much since your child was an infant and not an adult.

34. Some people really go out of their way to do nice things for you.

35. There are days when their existence almost feels like a dream.

FAQ About Grief and Child Loss

I have to admit, I knew nothing about child loss and real grief until I lost my child. I thought I knew something about it. I probably could have even spoken authoritatively on the subject, especially since I used to be a family therapist. I would have been wrong. I knew nothing.

After Toby died, some of my friends actually made a real effort to understand my grief. They Googled things and read pamphlets and kept up with my blog. I appreciated this. While this isn't anywhere near an exhaustive FAQ, I think it's a good start. I gathered these from all different kinds of sources. I have included many of them in the back of this book. Some of the answers made me feel less crazy.

How long does grief last?

Forever. Real grief never truly goes away. It becomes a part of you. Your feelings change and how you handle those feelings change, but the sadness and longing always remain. You might be able to find peace in your "new normal" and not break down crying every thirty minutes like you did in the past, but that doesn't mean that you're not still grieving the loss of your child.

Does everyone grieve the same?

No. Some people are vocal about their grief. Some people keep it to themselves. Some people might not feel the anger and resentment that others do. Some might feel guilt while others don't. No two people grieve the same, even though you might have shared the same loss.

Is it normal to feel like you're going crazy sometimes?

Yes. You might find that you're more forgetful than usual, that you have trouble making decisions, that you put your cell phone in the microwave...your brain is going through some really hard times trying to keep up with everything that's happening to you. The worst of this will pass in time.

Does infant loss bring all couples closer together?

Not always. Your partner is probably the closest person to you and, as such, is more than likely the person you have the most complex relationship with. You and your partner might grieve differently and not always be on the same page. You might also lash out at one another. Some couples work through their feelings through therapy. Others don't. Some couples find that their loss brings them closer together. Others find a wedge that is hard to close.

Can you control your grief?

No. You can't control your feelings but you can control your actions. There will be some fights that you just don't feel like fighting. There will be other ones that are far more important. Over time, some people find that they are able to "fake it until they make it." This isn't controlling their grief but it can be helpful to go through the motions sometimes so that the motions become easier. In the beginning, it might be hard to control your reactions to certain things and how you feel about them. This does tend to get better over time, though.

Why do you feel angry when you're grieving?

There are lots of reasons why anger is one of the strongest
emotions associated with grief. You might be angry at your
doctor for not preventing your child's death, angry at your
spouse for not being supportive enough, angry at your friends
for abandoning you, angry at yourself for not saving your child.
You might even be angry at your child sometimes, as crazy as
that sounds. Anger usually pops up when we feel out of control
and frustrated. And sometimes anger is totally justified.

Is it okay to feel okay?

There will come a time when you actually feel pretty good. This
might make you feel worse. The fact is, our minds need a break
from all the other emotions we feel. We have to give ourselves a
rest. As you move into another phase of your life your mind and
body will adjust, too, and this can give you a respite. This
doesn't mean that you are "over" your child's death. It just
means that your mind and body are dealing with it in a different
way.

What if I don't want to move on?

You don't have to. Moving on doesn't mean that you are over your child's death or that you are no longer grieving or sad. Sometimes, moving on simply means that you are facing a new reality and doing things a different way. I use the "parallel universe" theory to describe the way I feel about it. My husband says that he doesn't want to be the kind of man who could "move on" from his son's death. We will never be the same people. We choose to move forward, bringing our grief along with us. It doesn't mean that we're not sad or grieving, but it does mean that we are moving.

Why do I sometimes think I am okay and then I go out and suddenly find myself crying and overwhelmed?

This is something that Hospice refers to as a "grief spasm." It's basically a sudden shock of emotion that comes out of left field. Might last for an entire day or just a moment. It feels awful. But it's normal.

I thought I already went through the anger stage but now I am mad again. Why?

The stages of grief are not linear. You don't move through them and then bid farewell, never to see them again. They continue throughout the rest of your life and cycle. You will probably see all of them again at some point.

Support groups make me feel uncomfortable. Is there something wrong with me?

No. Not everyone feels comfortable talking about their feelings in front of a room full of strangers.

I don't want to attend counseling but everyone is pressuring me to go. Should I go?

Do you think you need to talk to someone? Counseling can be very helpful but it's ultimately up to you. If you don't go to counseling then finding another outlet can be a good idea. An online support group, for instance, might help. Or an in-person support group. Or journaling. Talking about your feelings or sharing them is beneficial but you don't have to do it publicly.

Other people are trying to convince me that my loss isn't as significant because my child was a baby. Am I wrong to feel so sad?

No. And those people have no idea what they're talking about.

I feel like I need medication to help me get through some of the rough times. Is that okay?

If you think you need some help then you should talk to your doctor. Do not feel like an addict because you need help after losing your child. If you feel depressed or have thoughts of suicide and your doctor won't help you then it's time to find another one.

Is it okay to talk to my friends about my grief?

You should have some friends that you feel comfortable talking to. Be aware that not all friends are going to be good listeners, though. Also be aware that, over time, even the best of friends might become weary. This can make you feel isolated and lonely. If friends don't want to talk to you at all then it might be time to reevaluate that friendship.

Is there a right way to grieve?

No.

My child died a month ago and I am still crying every day and having trouble functioning. Is there something wrong with me?

If you can get out of bed, eat, and have coherent thoughts then you are doing well. Actually, forget getting out of bed. If you can still eat and have coherent thoughts then you're still doing pretty well.

I want to have another child. Is it too soon?

Not if you think you're ready. Nobody else can make that decision for you.

Toby's Story

And now, here is my own story about my son's life and death.

The Birth

Toby was born on July 5, 2010. He was born just a few minutes short of being born on the 4th of July.

It was a very difficult pregnancy that ended four weeks early in a traumatic way. I had gone to my doctor on Friday, complaining of pain and extreme swelling. (You could barely tell it was me, my face was that swollen.) They sent me home, telling me I was fine. Less than 48 hours later I was gushing blood and hemorrhaging, thanks to a placental abruption and preeclampsia that had gone undetected. Luckily, we had gone away for the weekend to the next town over. Our hotel was downtown and just three blocks from one of the best hospitals in the country. I ended up having a complete placental abruption that ended in bloodbath and drama and had it happened two days earlier or two days later I don't think either one of us would have lived. At home, we were isolated in the country and the closest hospital to us would not have been equipped to take me. The time spent airlifting me to anywhere would have been detrimental.

We counted ourselves lucky.

1 week before having Toby

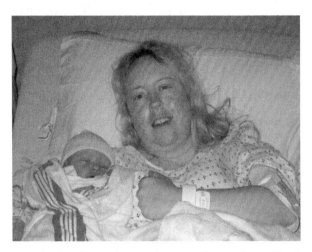

Day of Toby's birth-when my doctors said I was fine and had "no visible swelling"

I called my friends Becca and DeSha in the middle of the event to come and watch Sam for me while we were at the hospital. They left their 4th of July party and rushed over. Toby was born a little while later. The first thing I said to him was, "I promise things will get better."

We weren't allowed to have him that night because of the problems he had but that was really okay. I had lost a lot of blood and we were exhausted. Pete followed him to the NICU and videotaped him for me. I fell asleep and they woke me up the next morning and let me hold him.

He was perfect anyway

At home

Right away it was obvious that Toby was going to be a very sweet baby. He rarely cried and loved to cuddle. He was the exact opposite of Sam who had been demanding and was either crying or sleeping. The sleeping never lasted for long.

At home, Toby fit right in. I spent most of the day with him at home alone while Sam was at daycare. We watched our favorite TV shows together ("Full House", "Who's the Boss", and "The Gilmore Girls") and he helped me cook supper. I was going through a soup phase.

We took the kids on little picnics, to the fair, out to eat, for drives...Toby went a lot of places with me alone. Our favorite place was a little diner in Irvine where he would sleep and I would read and talk to the teenage waitress. She said that they loved it when he came in because he was so good and quiet. When Toby was two weeks old we took him to a writing retreat with us. He was great that weekend and barely made a peep. After Pete and I both participated in open mike one evening the woman in charge (our friend Kate Larken from Motes Books) said, "Wow, with parents like that he's going to have all kinds of talent."

293

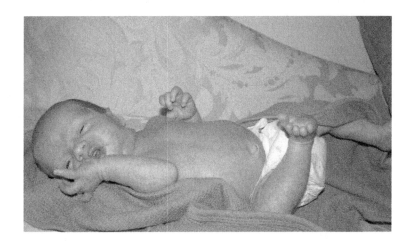

Changes

Not long after that, we saw a change in him. He got grumpy. He started crying a lot. It took them a year to diagnose Sam with severe acid reflux and I wasn't going to go through that again. Everyone had told us that when Sam cried it was because we spoiled him. Not true. It was because he was in pain. I took Toby to the doctor and he cried the whole time. The doctor recognized the reflux and gave him Zantac.

Around this time, I started getting weird symptoms, too. I started having panic attacks. Pain in my back and legs that had been associated with pregnancy got worse. My mind felt foggy and cloudy. There were some days that it was hard for me to get out of bed. I would shake and cry and not remember where I was. Now, we know that was part of my Chiari Malformation. Back then we didn't know.

One day, Mom and I took Toby out to eat. While she was holding him, he started convulsing. I tried to call my pediatrician. I talked to my nurse but she didn't seem concerned. In the car, it happened again. I got it on videotape.

The next day, I took him to the doctor. He was concerned and said that if it happened again he would send him to a neurologist.

My cousin was getting married in Nashville and we were afraid we would miss it. On the day before, though, I decided that I really wanted to go. We packed everyone up and headed to Nashville. It was so nice to see some of my family, like my Uncle Ray and Aunt Fran. Only two of my friends had met Toby at that point and we don't have family close so they hadn't met him, either. In fact, Toby died without even meeting my dad.

Hanging out, watching TV

The last weekend

Anyway, that was the last good weekend we would know for a
long time. We had so much fun with the kids. We took them
swimming and out to eat and to get ice cream. Toby cried a lot,
though. Aunt Fran urged me to take him back to the doctor. She
said something didn't seem right.

On the way back home we stopped at a sporting goods
store. We played in tents and pretended we were the Three Little
Pigs. We also ate at Cracker Barrel. People looked at us and
smiled and commented on what a nice looking family we were.

Unfortunately, I do not remember the rest of the week. Again, we thought it was PTSD. I was taking anti-anxiety medication but it wasn't helping. Now we know why.

On Friday afternoon my friend Karen came to visit. She got to meet Toby and spend about an hour with us. He laid on my chest most of the time. We were chilling on the couch. He was such a cuddlebunny.

That night, I went to bed early. I do not remember kissing him good night. I don't remember the last time I saw him. My last memory of him was around the time that Karen left. This is one of the worst parts.

A day of horror

The next morning, Mom and I were taking the kids to a literary event in Frankfort. I was supposed to get up early and get them dressed. Pete stayed up with Toby. I expected to be woken up around 6:00 am.

Instead, it was about 9:00 am when I woke up. Something didn't feel right. It felt too late. I peeked into our office where we had a spare bed and Pete was asleep. I thought he must have take Toby down to Mom to let me get some extra sleep. I used the quiet time to take a shower, put on some makeup. I had felt guilty about not spending as much time with the kids as I should have.

When I was ready, I woke Sam up. I took him downstairs and turned on cartoons for him. Then, I went in Mom's room to check on Toby and to see if she was ready. It was still so quiet. Mom was asleep, though, and alone.

I knew then that something was wrong.

I ran back upstairs and this time went all the way to the spare bed. Toby was blue and stiff. He had been gone for some time. I screamed and jumped on the bed and started doing CPR. Pete woke up and started screaming as well. After a few minutes I ran off to find my phone and call 911. Mom was up by then. I screamed at her, "He's dead, he's dead!" She grabbed her phone and we both ran back upstairs. She called 911 and took over doing CPR. Pete ran outside and grabbed Sam and stood in the yard to watch for the ambulance.

They were there in a matter of minutes which is crazy considering how far out we lived.

The paramedics picked him up in their arms and flew down the stairs. I followed them. One of them shouted, "Is this the mother?" and then pushed me into the ambulance.

A truck followed us and we pulled over in the middle of the highway. It was our neighbor. He was also a paramedic. He jumped in and we took off again. We needed the help.

At the local hospital they made me wait outside the door. Mom and Pete had not made it yet. I sat there alone and stared at the door. A few minutes later, the doctor came out and told me what I already knew.

At this point, they let me go into the room. A nurse was in there but everyone else cleared out. Toby was blue and red in some places. I stood next to him and cried and the nurse cried, too.

Mom, Pete, and Sam came in later. Pete had brought Toby's blanket for him. They thought he might still have a chance. I had to be the one to tell them he was gone. The staff played with Sam a little bit while we were all in the room with him.

Friends

When I got home our friends Becca and Rob were there. I had called them from the hospital and they had come to the house to wait for us. They had started to come to the hospital but wanted to stay at the house instead, to give us time with him alone.

Later, a few other friends showed up. They made me soup and helped me to bed. Mom and Ashley had taken the car seat out of the car, moved his swing out of the living room, and done a few other things so that I wouldn't be bombarded right away.

The coroner was there, too, to do an investigation. Becca said that he sat in the kitchen with Pete for an hour, convincing him it wasn't his fault. He said it was probably going to be labeled a SIDS death.

The next day, he called and left a detailed message. He said that although the autopsy wasn't complete, accidental suffocation had been ruled out.

I firmly believe that Toby would have died that night no matter what. I am glad Pete was with him. If he hadn't been lying next to Pete then he would have died, alone, in his crib. I am glad that the last thing he felt was Pete beside him.

Aftermath

People we knew and didn't know sent us cards, money for his headstone, and other gifts. Our friend Melissa had a yard sale to raise money for our expenses.

Unfortunately, we couldn't afford to take off any time from work. Toby died on a Saturday and Pete taught his classes on Monday. Eventually, I took about a week off. It just got too hard.

The first few months were spent in shock. About the time that people started telling us that we needed to "move on" was about the time that the real grief sunk in. The 6 month mark was probably the worst. His first birthday was sad. The milestones just kept getting harder.

I developed a form of agoraphobia after his death and had trouble leaving the house. Some people were very understanding of this and came out to visit us and hang out with us. Many people dropped off and we never saw them again. There were lots of changes in the aftermath of his death dealing with them could be just as hard as our grief.

Putting flowers on his brother's grave

We think about him every day and talk about him a lot. For us, he is still a part of our family and still here with us. His room decorations are used in our office. He gets a Christmas tree. We decorate his grave for the major holidays.

Toby was not here for very long, but he was still loved and he's still part of us.

Helpful Websites & Resources

Empty Arms Foundation

http://www.emptyarms.ca/index.php

(from their website) Empty Arms Foundation strives to achieve the following goals:

- Raise funds to assist in the research conducted by Dr. Hannah Kinney at Children's Hospital Boston
- Provide education about SIDS and separate fact from fiction
- Raise awareness of SIDS in the community
- Provide support to parents and family members grieving after the loss of a child
- Host regular charity events

Online Communities

Note: In many forums you will encounter people who have never lost babies to SIDS at all. They are simply there to either ask how they can "prevent" it (you can't, but you can reduce the risk) or they are there to tell you everything you did wrong. There are also those who get on the forums to tell everyone that their baby "almost died from SIDS." (Impossible. The name SIDS itself implies death. What they are referring to is an ALTE and that is completely different.) If you encounter these things on the board my advice is to walk away...

Daily Strength

http://www.dailystrength.org/c/Sudden-Infant-Death-Syndrome-SIDS/support-group

Daily Strength has one of the best active online SIDS support groups. It's been the one to hold me together. You can interact in the forums but also write your own journal entries that your friends can read. (Heck, if you think what I write on here is bad sometimes, you should see what I write in a more limited viewing community.)

Web Healing

http://webhealing.com/forums/

There is an active forum here, but like with many grief forums it can be hit and miss. You'd think that forums with people who have lost children would always be full of love. Mostly, they are. If you feel uncomfortable, just leave.

MedHelp

http://www.medhelp.org/forums/Sudden-Infant-Death-Syndrome-SIDS/show/205

MedHelp is a large website that has a lot of active members. The SIDS board isn't as active as the others but it might help you connect with other parents or at least read about others' experiences.

Other Websites

The Dougy Center

http://www.dougy.org/

The Grief Toolbox

http://thegrieftoolbox.com/

The Sudden Death of a Child

http://www.compassionatefriends.org/Brochures/sudden_death
_of_a_child.aspx

The Compassionate Friends Network has a brief, but kind of
spot-on, brochure describing the loss of a child. It's one of the
first things I read after Toby died.

First Candle

http://www.firstcandle.org/grieving-families/sids-suid/about-
sids-suid/

This is kind of THE resource for SIDS out there. It's a support
group/research foundation/information center...all in one. You
can learn about autopsies, dealing with grief, and SIDS in
general here.

SIDS Center

http://www.sidscenter.org/index.html

I don't always agree with their methods or lingo, but there is a
ton of information here. Some of it is not exactly user-friendly,
but if you are researching then you might want to start here.

American SIDS Institute

http://www.sids.org/

They often link to new research and studies that are out there.
Otherwise, their interface is simple and easy to manage so you
might have luck finding out the information you're looking for
easily.

Bereaved Parents of the USA

http://www.bereavedparentsusa.org/BP_Resources.htm

This site also has resources for grandparents and siblings, too.

The Cope Foundation

http://www.copefoundation.org/

This site is very comprehensive and one of my favorite things is called "The 10 Common Myths about Grief and Children." We forget sometimes that our other children are feeling grief, too.

Faith's Lodge

http://www.faithslodge.org/

This is an excellent place that has weekend retreats throughout the year, catering to parents who have lost children and other tragedies. The fee is almost non-existent and the setting is beautiful.

Compassionate Friends Network

http://www.compassionatefriends.org/home.aspx

This is a non-denominational support organization that has chapters all over the country. The website has a lot of helpful information and can also help you find a local chapter if you would like to attend a support group.

Movies About Child Death and Grieving

Rabbit Hole (2010)

The Greatest (2009)

Bridge to Terabithia (2007)

Moonlight Mile (2002)

Steel Magnolias (1989)

November Christmas (2010)

Lantana (2001)

The Other Woman (2009)

Blogs of Grieving Parents

Life After the Death of a Toddler

http://mamajamajenny.blogspot.com/

This Momma's Journey

http://thismommasjourney.blogspot.com/

Fireworks and Ferris Wheels

http://itscharlieovertheocean.blogspot.com/

Forever Our Angel

http://riverdaniel-foreverourangel.blogspot.com/

Jaden's Memories

http://jaydenalexander.blogspot.com/

Remembering Our Triplet Angels

http://rememberingourtripletangels.blogspot.com/

Colin's Corner

http://colinstuart.blogspot.com/

Holy Pee Stick Batman

http://holybfpbatman.blogspot.com/

Another Day Stronger

http://kandjstaats.blogspot.com/

Glow in the Woods

http://www.glowinthewoods.com/

Baby Macie

http://angelbabymacie.blogspot.com/

Hope Smiling Brightly

http://www.hopesmilingbrightly.com/

Acknowledgements

There are so many people that I need to thank that I could probably write an entirely separate book on just them. First, let's start with friends and family members.

I am eternally grateful for the family members who called, wrote, and stayed in touch with me after Toby's funeral. Special thanks goes to my Aunt Wilma who also lost a child.

There were several friends who went above and beyond the call of duty. Becca Morrison and Rob Day were very helpful in those first few weeks; cooking dinner, taking me to appointments, and generally helping to make things easier on us. Melissa Allen stuck by me when a lot of other people didn't and organized a yard sale for us. Writing friends, some of whom I had only met once, were incredibly loving to us. They sent cards and letters and messages and these things meant a lot to us. Special thanks to Kate Larken, Joette Morris Gates, Janine Musser, and Erin Fitzgerald.

I honestly do not think I could have made it without my online friends who are really so much more than simply "friends" at this point. These ladies and I share a bond that is horrible and wonderful at the same time. Many of them helped me with this book. These include: Karla Roy, Brandi Haefele,

Wanda Jewell, Becky Johnson, Kira Jackson, Stephanie Meyer-McClung, Julia Coleman, Michelle Chestnut, Brittany Watkins, Melissa Watkins, Jenny Nickell, and Willow. Special thanks to Katie Grant. She was the first bond I made and I sometimes refer to her as my "online BFF." Another special thanks to Valerie Megary who read over this with a fine eye for detail and gave me lots of excellent feedback.

Lastly, I would really like to thank my doctor Jennifer Shepherd. She stuck by me and was my biggest supporter as far as healthcare went. I really think that she and her nurses saved my life. Without them, I don't think that Toby would have survived his birth.

About Me

I am a full time writer and live in the mountains of Eastern Kentucky. My husband and I met in Wales where we were both doing our graduate studies. I brought him back to the United States with me and I consider him my most expensive souvenir. I am mother to two living children and one deceased child.

You can visit me at www.rebeccaphoward.com or my SIDS blog at www.lifeaftersids.blogspot.com

Made in the USA
Middletown, DE
07 August 2023